The Valley of

A Book of Romance and Some Old Tales

Henry Van Dyke

Alpha Editions

This edition published in 2024

ISBN : 9789362922588

Design and Setting By
Alpha Editions
www.alphaedis.com
Email - info@alphaedis.com

As per information held with us this book is in Public Domain.
This book is a reproduction of an important historical work. Alpha Editions uses the best technology to reproduce historical work in the same manner it was first published to preserve its original nature. Any marks or number seen are left intentionally to preserve its true form.

Contents

PREFACE .... - 1 -
A REMEMBERED DREAM .... - 2 -
ANTWERP ROAD .... - 7 -
A CITY OF REFUGE .... - 9 -
A SANCTUARY OF TREES .... - 15 -
THE KING'S HIGH WAY .... - 27 -
HALF-TOLD TALES .... - 31 -
THE TRAITOR IN THE HOUSE .... - 33 -
JUSTICE OF THE ELEMENTS .... - 35 -
ASHES OF VENGEANCE .... - 36 -
THE BROKEN SOLDIER AND THE MAID OF FRANCE .- 39 -
   I. THE MEETING AT THE SPRING .... - 41 -
   II. THE GREEN CONFESSIONAL .... - 46 -
   III. THE ABSOLVING DREAM .... - 54 -
   IV. THE VICTORIOUS PENANCE .... - 60 -
THE HEARING EAR .... - 63 -
SKETCHES OF QUEBEC .... - 71 -
A CLASSIC INSTANCE .... - 80 -
HALF-TOLD TALES .... - 91 -
THE NEW ERA AND CARRY ON .... - 93 -
THE PRIMITIVE AND HIS SANDALS .... - 95 -
DIANA AND THE LIONS .... - 98 -
THE HERO AND TIN SOLDIERS .... - 102 -
SALVAGE POINT .... - 105 -
THE BOY OF NAZARETH DREAMS .... - 112 -
   I. THE JOURNEY TO THE CITY .... - 113 -

II. THE GILDED TEMPLE .... - 118 -
III. HOW THE BOY WAS LOST .... - 121 -
IV. HOW THE BOY WENT HIS WAY .... - 125 -
V. HOW THE BOY WAS FOUND .... - 132 -

PREFACE

"Why do you choose such a title as *The Valley of Vision* for your book," said my friend; "do you mean that one can see farther from the valley than from the mountain-top?"

This question set me thinking, as every honest question ought to do. Here is the result of my thoughts, which you will take for what it is worth, if you care to read the book.

The mountain-top is the place of outlook over the earth and the sea. But it is in the valley of suffering, endurance, and self-sacrifice that the deepest visions of the meaning of life come to us.

I take the outcome of this Twentieth Century War as a victory over the mad illusion of world-dominion which the Germans saw from the peak of their military power in 1914. The united force of the Allies has grown, through valley-visions of right and justice and human kindness, into an irresistible might before which the German "will to power" has gone down in ruin.

There are some Half-Told Tales in the volume—fables, fantasies—mere sketches, grave and gay, on the margin of the book of life,

> *"Where more is meant than meets the ear."*

Dreams have a part in most of the longer stories. That is because I believe dreams have a part in real life. Some of them we remember as vividly as any actual experience. These belong to the imperfect sleep. But others we do not remember, because they are given to us in that perfect sleep in which the soul is liberated, and goes visiting. Yet sometimes we get a trace of them, by a happy chance, and often their influence remains with us in that spiritual refreshment with which we awake from profound slumber. This is the meaning of that verse in the old psalm: "He giveth to His beloved in sleep."

The final story in the book was written before the War of 1914 began, and it has to do with the Light of the World, leading us through conflict and suffering towards Peace.

AVALON, November 24, 1918.

A REMEMBERED DREAM

This is the story of a dream that came to me some five-and-twenty years ago. It is as vivid in memory as anything that I have ever seen in the outward world, as distinct as any experience through which I have ever passed. Not all dreams are thus remembered. But some are. In the records of the mind, where the inner chronicle of life is written, they are intensely clear and veridical. I shall try to tell the story of this dream with an absolute faithfulness, adding nothing and leaving nothing out, but writing the narrative just as if the thing were real.

Perhaps it was. Who can say?

In the course of a journey, of the beginning and end of which I know nothing, I had come to a great city, whose name, if it was ever told me, I cannot recall.

It was evidently a very ancient place. The dwelling-houses and larger buildings were gray and beautiful with age, and the streets wound in and out among them wonderfully, like a maze.

This city lay beside a river or estuary—though that was something that I did not find out until later, as you will see—and the newer part of the town extended mainly on a wide, bare street running along a kind of low cliff or embankment, where the basements of the small houses on the water-side went down, below the level of the street, to the shore. But the older part of the town was closely and intricately built, with gabled roofs and heavy carved facades hanging over the narrow stone-paved ways, which here and there led out suddenly into open squares.

It was in what appeared to be the largest and most important of these squares that I was standing, a little before midnight. I had left my wife and our little girl in the lodging which we had found, and walked out alone to visit the sleeping town.

The night sky was clear, save for a few filmy clouds, which floated over the face of the full moon, obscuring it for an instant, but never completely hiding it—like veils in a shadow dance. The spire of the great cathedral was silver filigree on the moonlit side, and on the other side, black lace. The square was empty. But on the broad, shallow steps in front of the main entrance of the cathedral two heroic figures were seated. At first I thought they were statues. Then I perceived they were alive, and talking earnestly together.

They were like Greek gods, very strong and beautiful, and naked but for some slight drapery that fell snow-white around them. They glistened in the moonlight. I could not hear what they were saying; yet I could see that they were in a dispute which went to the very roots of life.

They resembled each other strangely in form and feature—like twin brothers. But the face of one was noble, lofty, calm, full of a vast regret and compassion. The face of the other was proud, resentful, drawn with passion. He appeared to be accusing and renouncing his companion, breaking away from an ancient friendship in a swift, implacable hatred. But the companion seemed to plead with him, and lean toward him, and try to draw him closer.

A strange fear and sorrow shook my heart. I felt that this mysterious contest was something of immense importance; a secret, ominous strife; a menace to the world.

Then the two figures stood up, marvellously alike in strength and beauty, yet absolutely different in expression and bearing, the one serene and benignant, the other fierce and threatening. The quiet one was still pleading, with a hand laid upon the other's shoulder. But he shook it off, and thrust his companion away with a proud, impatient gesture.

At last I heard him speak.

"I have done with you," he cried. "I do not believe in you. I have no more need of you. I renounce you. I will live without you. Away forever out of my life!"

At this a look of ineffable sorrow and pity came upon the great companion's face.

"You are free," he answered. "I have only besought you, never constrained you. Since you will have it so, I must leave you, now, to yourself."

He rose into the air, still looking downward with wise eyes full of grief and warning, until he vanished in silence beyond the thin clouds.

The other did not look up, but lifting his head with a defiant laugh, shook his shoulders as if they were free of a burden. He strode swiftly around the corner of the cathedral and disappeared among the deep shadows.

A sense of intolerable calamity fell upon me. I said to myself:

"That was Man! And the other was God! And they have parted!"

Then the multitude of bells hidden in the lace-work of the high tower began to sound. It was not the aerial fluttering music of the carillon that I remembered hearing long ago from the belfries of the Low Countries. This was a confused and strident ringing, jangled and broken, full of sudden tumults and discords, as if the tower were shaken and the bells gave out their notes at hazard, in surprise and trepidation.

It stopped as suddenly as it began. The great bell of the hours struck twelve. The windows of the cathedral glowed faintly with a light from within.

"It is New Year's Eve," I thought—although I knew perfectly well that the time was late summer. I had seen that though the leaves on the trees of the square were no longer fresh, they had not yet fallen.

I was certain that I must go into the cathedral. The western entrance was shut. I hurried to the south side. The dark, low door of the transept was open. I went in. The building was dimly lighted by huge candles which flickered and smoked like torches. I noticed that one of them, fastened against a pillar, was burning crooked, and the tallow ran down its side in thick white tears.

The nave of the church was packed with a vast throng of people, all standing, closely crowded together, like the undergrowth in a forest. The rood-screen was open, or broken down, I could not tell which. The choir was bare, like a clearing in the woods, and filled with blazing light.

On the high steps, with his back to the altar, stood Man, his face gleaming with pride.

"I am the Lord!" he cried. "There is none above me! No law, no God! Man is power. Man is the highest of all!"

A tremor of wonder and dismay, of excitement and division, shivered through the crowd. Some covered their faces. Others stretched out their hands. Others shook their fists in the air. A tumult of voices broke from the multitude—voices of exultation, and anger, and horror, and strife.

The floor of the cathedral was moved and lifted by a mysterious ground-swell. The pillars trembled and wavered. The candles flared and went out. The crowd, stricken dumb with a panic fear, rushed to the doors, burst open the main entrance, and struggling in furious silence poured out of the building. I was swept along with them, striving to keep on my feet.

One thought possessed me. I must get to my wife and child, save them, bring them out of this accursed city.

As I hurried across the square I looked up at the cathedral spire. It was swaying and rocking in the air like the mast of a ship at sea. The lace-work fell from it in blocks of stone. The people rushed screaming through the rain of death. Many were struck down, and lay where they fell.

I ran as fast as I could. But it was impossible to run far. Every street and alley vomited men—all struggling together, fighting, shouting, or shrieking, striking one another down, trampling over the fallen—a hideous melee. There was an incessant rattling noise in the air, and heavier peals as of thunder shook the houses. Here a wide rent yawned in a wall—there a roof caved in—the windows fell into the street in showers of broken glass.

How I got through this inferno I do not know. Buffeted and blinded, stumbling and scrambling to my feet again, turning this way or that way to avoid the thickest centres of the strife, oppressed and paralyzed by a feeling of impotence that put an iron band around my heart, driven always by the intense longing to reach my wife and child, somehow I had a sense of struggling on. Then I came into a quieter quarter of the town, and ran until I reached the lodging where I had left them.

They were waiting just inside the door, anxious and trembling. But I was amazed to find them so little panic-stricken. The little girl had her doll in her arms.

{Illustration with caption: The cathedral spire... was swaying and rocking in the air like the mast of a ship at sea.} "What is it?" asked my wife. "What must we do?"

"Come," I cried. "Something frightful has happened here. I can't explain now. We must get away at once. Come, quickly."

Then I took a hand of each and we hastened through the streets, vaguely steering away from the centre of the city.

Presently we came into that wide new street of mean houses, of which I have already spoken. There were a few people in it, but they moved heavily and feebly, as if some mortal illness lay upon them. Their faces were pale and haggard with a helpless anxiety to escape more quickly. The houses seemed half deserted. The shades were drawn, the doors closed.

But since it was all so quiet, I thought that we might find some temporary shelter there. So I knocked at the door of a house where there was a dim light behind the drawn shade in one of the windows.

After a while the door was opened by a woman who held the end of her shawl across her mouth. All that I could see was the black sorrow of her eyes.

"Go away," she said slowly; "the plague is here. My children are dying of it. You must not come in! Go away."

So we hurried on through that plague-smitten street, burdened with a new fear. Soon we saw a house on the riverside which looked absolutely empty. The shades were up, the windows open, the door stood ajar. I hesitated; plucked up courage; resolved that we must get to the waterside in some way in order to escape from the net of death which encircled us.

"Come," I said, "let us try to go down through this house. But cover your mouths."

We groped through the empty passageway, and down the basement-stair. The thick cobwebs swept my face. I noted them with joy, for I thought they proved that the house had been deserted for some time, and so perhaps it might not be infected.

We descended into a room which seemed to have been the kitchen. There was a stove dimly visible at one side, and an old broken kettle on the floor, over which we stumbled. The back door was locked. But it swung outward as I broke it open. We stood upon a narrow, dingy beach, where the small waves were lapping.

By this time the "little day" had begun to whiten the eastern sky; a pallid light was diffused; I could see westward down to the main harbor, beside the heart of the city. The sails and smoke-stacks of great ships were visible, all passing out to sea. I wished that we were there.

Here in front of us the water seemed shallower. It was probably only a tributary or backwater of the main stream. But it was sprinkled with smaller vessels—sloops, and yawls, and luggers—all filled with people and slowly creeping seaward.

There was one little boat, quite near to us, which seemed to be waiting for some one. There were some people on it, but it was not crowded.

"Come," I said, "this is for us. We must wade out to it."

So I took my wife by the hand, and the child in the other arm, and we went into the water. Soon it came up to our knees, to our waists.

"Hurry," shouted the old man at the tiller. "No time to spare!"

"Just a minute more," I answered, "only one minute!"

That minute seemed like a year. The sail of the boat was shaking in the wind. When it filled she must move away. We waded on, and at last I grasped the gunwale of the boat. I lifted the child in and helped my wife to climb over the side. They clung to me. The little vessel began to move gently away.

"Get in," cried the old man sharply; "get in quick."

But I felt that I could not, I dared not. I let go of the boat. I cried "Good-by," and turned to wade ashore.

I was compelled to go back to the doomed city. I must know what would come of the parting of Man from God!

The tide was running out more swiftly. The water swirled around my knees. I awoke.

But the dream remained with me, just as I have told it to you.

ANTWERP ROAD

{OCTOBER, 1914}

Along the straight, glistening road, through a dim arcade of drooping trees, a tunnel of faded green and gold, dripping with the misty rain of a late October afternoon, a human tide was flowing, not swiftly, but slowly, with the patient, pathetic slowness of weary feet, and numb brains, and heavy hearts.

Yet they were in haste, all of these old men and women, fathers and mothers, and little children; they were flying as fast as they could; either away from something that they feared, or toward something that they desired.

That was the strange thing—the tide on the road flowed in two directions.

Some fled away from ruined homes to escape the perils of war. Some fled back to ruined homes to escape the desolation of exile. But all were fugitives, anxious to be gone, striving along the road one way or the other, and making no more speed than a creeping snail's pace of unutterable fatigue. I saw many separate things in the tide, and remembered them without noting.

A boy straining to push a wheelbarrow with his pale mother in it, and his two little sisters trudging at his side. A peasant with his two girls driving their lean, dejected cows back to some unknown pasture. A bony horse tugging at a wagon heaped high with bedding and household gear, on top of which sat the wrinkled grandmother with the tiniest baby in her arms, while the rest of the family stumbled alongside—and the cat was curled up on the softest coverlet in the wagon. Two panting dogs, with red tongues hanging out, and splayed feet clawing the road, tugging a heavy-laden cart while the master pushed behind and the woman pulled in the shafts. Strange, antique vehicles crammed with passengers. Couples and groups and sometimes larger companies of foot-travellers. Now and then a solitary man or woman, old and shabby, bundle on back, eyes on the road, plodding through the mud and the mist, under the high archway of yellowing leaves.

{Illustration: All were fugitives, anxious to be gone, ... and making no more speed than a creeping snail's pace of unutterable fatigue.}

All these distinct pictures I saw, yet it was all one vision—a vision of humanity with its dumb companions in flight—infinitely slow, painful, pitiful flight!

I saw no tears, I heard no cries of complaint. But beneath the numb and patient haste on all those dazed faces I saw a question.

"What have we done? Why has this thing come upon us and our children?"

Somewhere I heard a trumpet blown. The brazen spikes on the helmets of a little troop of German soldiers flashed for an instant, far down the sloppy road. Through the humid dusk came the dull, distant booming of the unseen guns of conquest in Flanders.

That was the only answer.

A CITY OF REFUGE

In the dark autumn of 1914 the City sprang up almost in a night, as if by enchantment.

It was white magic that called it into being—the deep, quiet, strong impulse of compassion and protection that moved the motherly heart of Holland when she saw the hundreds of thousands of Belgian fugitives pouring out of their bleeding, ravaged land, and running, stumbling, creeping on hands and knees, blindly, instinctively turning to her for safety and help.

"Come to me," she said, like a good woman who holds out her arms and spreads her knees to make a lap for tired and frightened children, "come to me. I will take care of you. You shall be safe with me."

All doors were open. The little brick farmhouses and cottages with their gayly painted window-shutters; the long rows of city houses with their steep gables; the prim and placid country mansions set among their high trees and formal flower-gardens—all kinds of dwellings, from the poorest to the richest, welcomed these guests of sorrow and distress. Many a humble family drained its savings-bank reservoir to keep the stream of its hospitality flowing. Unused factories were turned into barracks. Deserted summer hotels were filled up. Even empty greenhouses were adapted to the need of human horticulture. All Holland was enrolled, formally or informally, in a big *Comite voor Belgische Slachtoffers*.

But soon it was evident that the impromptu methods of generosity could not meet the demands of the case. Private resources were exhausted. Poor people could no longer feed and clothe their poorer guests. Families were unhappily divided. In the huge flock of exiles driven out by the cruel German Terror there were goats as well as sheep, and some of them bewildered and shocked the orderly Dutch homes where they were sheltered, by their nocturnal habits and negligible morals. Something had to be done to bring order and system into the chaos of brotherly love. Otherwise the neat Dutch mind which is so close to the Dutch heart could not rest in its bed. This vast trouble which the evil of German militarism had thrust upon a helpless folk must be helped out by a wise touch of military organization, which is a good thing even for the most peaceful people.

So it was that the City of Refuge (and others like it) grew up swiftly in the wilderness.

It stands in the heathland that slopes and rolls from the wooded hills of Gelderland to the southern shore of the Zuider Zee—a sandy country overgrown with scrub-oaks and pines and heather—yet very healthy and well drained, and not unfertile under cultivation. You may see that in the little neighbor-village, where the trees arch over the streets, and the kitchen-gardens prosper, and the shrubs and flowers bloom abundantly.

The small houses and hotels of this tiny summer resort are of brick. It has an old, well-established look; a place of relaxation with restraint, not of ungirdled frivolity. The plain Dutch people love their holidays, but they take them serenely and by rule: long walks and bicycle-rides, placid and nourishing picnics in the woods or by the sea, afternoon tea-parties in sheltered arbors. One of their favorite names for a country-place is *Wel Teweden,* "perfectly contented."

The commandant of the City of Refuge lives in one of the little brick houses of the village. He is a portly, rosy old bachelor, with a curly brown beard and a military bearing; a man of fine education and wide experience, seasoned in colonial diplomacy. The ruling idea in his mind is discipline, authority. His official speech is abrupt and final, the manner of a martinet covering a heart full of kindness and generous impulses.

"Come," he says, after a good breakfast, "I want you to see my camp. It is not as fine and fancy as the later ones. But we built it in a hurry and we had it ready on time."

A short ride over a sandy road brings you to the city gate—an opening in the wire enclosure of perhaps two or three square miles among the dwarf pines and oaks. The guard-house is kept by a squad of Dutch soldiers. But it is in no sense a prison-camp, for people are coming and going freely all the time, and the only rules within are those of decency and good order.

"Capacity, ten thousand," says the commandant, sweeping his hand around the open circle, "quite a city, *niet waar?* I will show you the various arrangements."

All the buildings are of wood, a mushroom city, but constructed with intelligence to meet the needs of the sudden, helpless population. You visit the big kitchen with its ever-simmering kettles; the dining-halls with their long tables and benches; the schoolhouses full of lively, irrepressible children; the wash-house where always talkative and jocose laundresses are scrubbing and wringing the clothes; the sewing-rooms where hundreds of women and girls are busy with garments and gossip; the chapel where religious services are held by the devoted pastors; the recreation-room which is the social centre of the city; the clothing storerooms where you find several American girls working for love.

Then you go through the long family barracks where each family has a separate cubicle, more or less neat and comfortable, sometimes prettily decorated, according to the family taste and habit; the barracks for the single men; the barracks for the single women; the two hospitals, one general, the other for infectious diseases; and last of all, the house where the half-dozen disorderly women are confined, surrounded by a double fence of barbed wire and guarded by a sentry.

Poor, wretched creatures! You are sorry for them. Why not put the disorderly men into a house of confinement, too?

"Ah," says the commandant bluntly, "we find it easier and better to send the disorderly men to jail or hospital in some near town. We are easier with the women. I pity them. But they are full of poison. We can't let them go loose in the camp for fear of infection."

How many of the roots of human nature are uncovered in a place like this! The branches and the foliage and the blossoms, too, are seen more clearly in this air where all things are necessarily open and in common.

The men are generally less industrious than the women. But they work willingly at the grading of roads and paths, the laying out and planting of flower-beds, the construction of ornamental designs, of doubtful taste but unquestionable sincerity.

You read the names which they have given to the different streets and barracks, and the passageways between the cubicles, and you understand the strong, instinctive love which binds them to their native Belgium. "Antwerp Avenue," "Louvain Avenue," "Malines Street," "Liege Street," and streets bearing the names of many ruined towns and villages of which you have never heard, but which are forever dear to the hearts of these exiles. The names of the hero-king, Albert, and of his brave consort, Queen Elizabeth, are honored by inscriptions, and their pictures, cut from, newspapers, decorate the schoolrooms and the little family cubicles.

The brutal power which reigns at Berlin may drive the Belgians out of Belgium by terror and oppression. But it cannot drive Belgium out of the hearts of the Belgians. While they live their country lives, and Albert is still their King.

But think of the unnatural conditions into which these thousands of human beings—yes, and hundreds of thousands like them, torn from their homes, uprooted, dispersed, impoverished—are forced by this bitter, cruel war. Think of the cold and ruined hearthstones, the scattered families, the shelterless children, the desolate and broken hearts. This is what Germany has inflicted upon mankind in order to realize her robber-dream!

Yet the City of Refuge, being human, has its bright spots and its bits of compensation. Here is one, out of many.

The chief nurse, a young Dutch lady of charming face and manners, serving as a volunteer under the sacred sign of the Red Cross, comes in, one morning, to make her report to the commandant.

"Well," he says, disguising in his big voice of command the warm admiration which he feels for the lady, "what is the trouble to-day? Speak up."

"Nothing, sir," she answers calmly. "Everything is going on pretty well. No new cases of measles—those in hospital improving. The only thing that bothers me is the continual complaint about that Mrs. Van Orley—you remember her, a thin, dark little person. She is melancholy and morose, quarrels all the time, says some one has stolen her children. The people near her in the barracks complain that she disturbs them at night, moans and talks aloud in her sleep, jumps up and runs down the corridor laughing or crying: 'Here they are!' They don't believe she ever had any children. They think she is crazy and want her put out. But I don't agree with that. I think she has had children, and now she has dreams."

"Send her away," growls the commandant; "send her to a sanatorium! This camp is not a lunatic asylum."

"But," interposes the nurse in her most discreet voice, "she is really a very nice woman. If you would allow me to take her on as a housemaid in the general hospital, I think I could make something out of her; at least I should like to try."

"Have your own way," says the commandant, relenting; "you always do. Now tell me the next trouble. You have something more up your sleeve, I'm sure."

"Babies," she replies demurely; "two babies from Amsterdam. Lost, somehow or other, in the flight. No trace of their people. A family in Zaandam has been taking care of them, but can't afford it any longer. So the Amsterdam committee has sent them here."

The commandant has listened, his cheeks growing redder and redder, his eyes rounder and more prominent. He springs up and paces the floor in wrath.

"Babies!" he cries stormily. "By all the gods, da—those Amsterdammers! Excuse me, but this is too much. Do they think this is a foundling asylum? or a nursing home? Babies! What in Heaven's name am I to do with them? Babies! Where are those babies?"

"Just outside, and very nice babies indeed," says the nurse, opening the hall door and giving a soft call.

Enter a slim black-haired boy of about three and a half years and a plump golden-haired girl about a year younger. They toddle to the nurse and snuggle against her blue dress and white apron.

Smiling she guides them toward the commandant and says: "Here they are, sir. How do you like them?"

That terrific personage has been suddenly transformed from haircloth into silk. He beams, and pulling out his fat gold watch, coos like a hoarse dove: "Look here, *kinderen*, come and hear the bells in my tick-tock!"

Presently he has one of them leaning against the inside of each knee, listening ardently to the watch.

"What do you think of that!" he says. "What is your name, youngster?"

"Hendrik," answers the boy, looking up.

"Hendrik *what*? You have another name, haven't you?"

The boy shakes his head and looks puzzled, as if the thought of two names were too much for him. *"Hendrik,"* he repeats more clearly and firmly.

"And what is her name?" asks the commandant, patting the little girl.

"Sooss," answers the boy. "Mama say *'ickle angel.'* Hendrik say *Sooss.*"

All effort to get any more information from the children was fruitless. They were too small to remember much, and what they did remember was of their own size—only very little things, of no importance except to themselves. The commandant looks at the nurse quizzically.

"Now, miss, you have unloaded these vague babies on me. What do you propose that I should do with them? Adopt them?"

"Not yet, anyhow," she answers, smiling broadly. "Let us take them up to the camp. I'll bet we can find some one there to look after them. What do you say, sir?"

"Well, well," he sighs, "have your own way as usual! Just ring that bell for the automobile, *als't-Ublieft.*"

In the busy sewing-room the two children are standing up on one of the tables. The commandant has an arm around each of them, for they are a little frightened by so much noise and so many eyes looking at them. The chatter dies down, as he speaks in his gruff authoritative voice, but with a twinkle in his eyes, rather like a middle-aged Santa Claus.

"Look here! I've got two fine babies."

A titter runs through the room.

"*Ja, Men'eer,*" says one of the women, "congratulations! They are *lievelingen*—darlings!"

"Silence!" growls the commandant amiably. "None of your impudence, you women. Look here! These two children—I want somebody to adopt them, or at least to take care of them. I will pay for them. Their names are Hendrik and—"

A commotion at the lower end of the room. A thin, dark little woman is standing up, waving her piece of sewing like a flag, her big eyes flaming with excitement.

"Stop!" she cries, hurrying and stumbling forward through the crowd of women and girls. "Oh, stop a minute! They are mine—I lost them—mine, I tell you—lost—mine!"

She reaches the head of the table and flings her arms around the boy, crying: "My Hendrik!"

The boy hesitates a second, startled by the sudden wildness of her caress. Then he presses his hot little face in her neck.

"*Lieve moeder!*" he murmurs. "Where was you? I looked."

But the thin, dark little woman has fainted dead away.

The rest we will leave, as the wise commandant does, to the chief nurse.

A SANCTUARY OF TREES

The Baron d'Azan was old—older even than his seventy years. His age showed by contrast as he walked among his trees. They were fresh and flourishing, full of sap and vigor, though many of them had been born long before him.

The tracts of forest which still belonged to his diminished estate were crowded with the growths native to the foot-hills of the Ardennes. In the park around the small chateau, built in a Belgian version of the First Empire style, trees from many lands had been assembled by his father and grandfather: drooping spruces from Norway, dark-pillared cypresses from Italy, spreading cedars from Lebanon, trees of heaven from China, fern-leaved gingkos from Japan, lofty tulip-trees and liquidambars from America, and fantastic sylvan forms from islands of the Southern Ocean. But the royal avenue of beeches! Well, I must tell you more about that, else you can never feel the meaning of this story.

The love of trees was hereditary in the family and antedated their other nobility. The founder of the house had begun life as the son of a forester in Luxemburg. His name was Pol Staar. His fortune and title were the fruit of contracts for horses and provisions which he made with the commissariat of Napoleon I. in the days when the Netherlands were a French province. But though Pol Staar's hands were callous and his manners plain, his tastes were aristocratic. They had been formed young in the company of great trees.

Therefore when he bought his estate of Azan (and took his title from it) he built his chateau in a style which he considered complimentary to his imperial patron, but he was careful also to include within his domain large woodlands in which he could renew the allegiance of his youth. These woodlands he cherished and improved, cutting with discretion, planting with liberality, and rejoicing in the thought that trees like those which had befriended his boyhood would give their friendly protection to his heirs. These are traits of an aristocrat—attachment to the past, and careful provision for posterity. It was in this spirit that Pol Staar, first Baron d'Azan, planted in 1809 the broad avenue of beeches, leading from the chateau straight across the park to the highroad. But he never saw their glory, for he died when they were only twenty years old.

His son and successor was of a different timber and grain; less aristocratic, more bourgeois—a rover, a gambler, a man of fashion. He migrated from the gaming-tables at Spa to the Bourse at Paris, perching at many clubs between and beyond, and making seasonal nests in several places. This left him little time for the Chdteau d'Azan. But he came there every spring and autumn, and showed the family fondness for trees in his own fashion. He loved the forests so much that he ate them. He cut with liberality and planted without discretion. But for the great avenue of beeches he had a saving admiration. Not even to support the gaming-table would he have allowed them to be felled.

When he turned the corner of his thirty-first year he had a sharp illness, a temporary reformation, and brought home as his wife a very young lovely actress from the ducal theatre at Saxe-Meiningen. She was a good girl, deeply in love with her handsome husband, to whom she bore a son and heir in the first year of their marriage. Not many moons thereafter the pleased but restless father slid back into his old rounds again. The forest waned and the debts waxed. Rumors of wild doings came from Spa and Aix, from Homburg and Baden, from Trouville and Ostend. After four years of this the young mother died, of no namable disease, unless you call it heart-failure, and the boy was left to his grandmother's care and company among the trees.

Every day when it was fair the old lady and the little lad took their afternoon walk together in the beech-tree avenue, where the tips of the branches now reached the road. At other times he roamed the outlying woods and learned to know the birds and the little wild animals. When he was twelve his grandmother died. After that he was left mainly to the housekeeper, his tutors, and the few friends he could make among the children of the neighborhood.

When he had finished his third year at the University of Louvain and attained his majority, his father returned express-haste from somewhere in Bohemia, to attend the coronation of Leopold II, that remarkable King of Belgium and the Bourse. But by this time the gay Baron d'Azan had become stout, the pillar of his neck seemed shorter because it was thicker, and the rose in his bold cheek had the purplish tint of a crimson rambler. So he died of an apoplexy during the festivities, and his son brought him back to the Chateau d'Azan, and buried him there with due honor, and mourned for him as was fitting. Thus Albert, third Baron d'Azan, entered upon his inheritance.

It seemed, at first, to consist mainly of debts. These were paid by the sale of the deforested lands and of certain detached woodlands. By the same method, much as he disliked it, he made a modest provision of money for continuing his education and beginning his travels. He knew that he had much to learn of the world, and he was especially desirous of pursuing his favorite study of botany, which a wise old priest at Louvain had taught him to love. So he engaged an intelligent and faithful forester to care for the trees and the estate, closed the house, and set forth on his journeys.

They led him far and wide. In the course of them no doubt he studied other things than botany. It may be that he sowed some of the wild oats with which youth is endowed; but not in the gardens of others; nor with that cold self-indulgence which transforms passionate impulse into sensual habit. He had a permanent and regulative devotion to botanical research; and that is a study which seems to promote modesty, tranquillity, and steadiness of mind in its devotees, of whom the great Linnaeus is the shining exemplar. Young Albert d'Azan sat at the feet of the best masters in Europe and America. He crossed the western continent to observe the oldest of living things, the giant Sequoias of California. He went to Australasia and the Dutch East Indies and South America in search of new ferns and orchids. He investigated the effect of ocean currents and of tribal migrations in the distribution of trees. His botanical monographs brought him renown among those who know, and he was elected a corresponding member of many scientific societies. After twenty years of voyaging he returned to port at Azan, richly laden with observation and learning, and settled down among his trees to pursue his studies and write his books.

The estate, under the forester's care, had improved a little and promised a modest income. The house, though somewhat dilapidated, was easily made livable. But the one thing that was full of glory and splendor, triumphantly prosperous, was the great avenue of beeches. Their long, low aisle of broad arches was complete. They shimmered with a pearly mist of buds in early spring and later with luminous green of tender leafage. In mid-summer they formed a wide, still stream of dark, unruffled verdure; in autumn they were transmuted through glowing yellow into russet gold; in winter their massy trunks were pillars of gray marble and the fan-tracery of their rounded branches was delicately etched against the sky.

"Look at them," the baron would say to the guests whom the fame of his learning and the charm of his wide-ranging conversation often brought to his house. "Those beeches were planted by my grandfather after the battle of Wagram, when Napoleon whipped the Austrians. After that came the Beresina and Leipsic and Waterloo and how many battles and wars of furious, perishable men. Yet the trees live on peaceably, they unfold their strength in beauty, they have not yet reached the summit of their grandeur. We are all *parvenus* beside them."

"If you had to choose," asked the great sculptor Constantin Meunier one day, "would you have your house or one of these trees struck by lightning?"

"The house," answered the botanist promptly, "for I could rebuild it in a year; but to restore the tree would take three-quarters of a century."

"Also," said the sculptor, with a smile, "you might change the style of your house with advantage, but the style of these trees you could never improve."

"But tell me," he continued, "is it true, as they say, that lightning never strikes a beech?"

"It is not entirely true," replied the botanist, smiling in his turn, "yet, like many ancient beliefs, it has some truth in it. There is something in the texture of the beech that seems to resist electricity better than other trees. It may be the fatness of the wood. Whatever it is, I am glad of it, for it gives my trees a better chance."

"Don't be too secure," said the sculptor, shaking his head. "There are other tempests besides those in the clouds. When the next war comes in western Europe Belgium will be the battle-field. Beech-wood is very good to burn."

"God forbid," said the baron devoutly. "We have had peace for a quarter of a century. Why should it not last?"

"Ask the wise men of the East," replied the sculptor grimly.

When he was a little past fifty the baron married, with steadfast choice and deep affection, the orphan daughter of a noble family of Hainault. She was about half his age; of a tranquil, cheerful temper and a charm that depended less on feature than on expression; a lover of music, books, and a quiet life. She brought him a small dowry by which the chateau was restored to comfort, and bore him two children, a boy and a girl, by whom it was enlivened with natural gayety. The next twenty years were the happiest that Albert d'Azan and his wife ever saw. The grand avenue of beeches became to them the unconscious symbol of something settled and serene, august, protective, sacred.

On a brilliant morning of early April, 1914, they had stepped out together to drink the air. The beeches were in misty, silver bloom above them. All around was peace and gladness.

"I want to tell you a dream I had last night," he said, "a strange dream about our beeches."

"If it was sad," she answered, "do not let the shadow of it fall on the morning."

"But it was not sad. It seemed rather to bring light and comfort. I dreamed that I was dead and you had buried me at the foot of the largest of the trees."

"Do you call that not sad?" she interrupted reproachfully.

"It did not seem so. Wait a moment and you shall hear the way of it. At first I felt only a deep quietness and repose, like one who has been in pain and is very tired and lies down in the shade to sleep. Then I was waking again and something was drawing me gently upward. I cannot exactly explain it, but it was as if I were passing through the roots and the trunk and the boughs of the beech-tree toward the upper air. There I saw the light again and heard the birds singing and the wind rustling among the leaves. How I saw and heard I cannot tell you, for there was no remembrance of a body in my dream. Then suddenly my soul—I suppose it was that—stood before God and He was asking me: 'How did you come hither?' I answered, 'By Christ's way, by the way of a tree.' And He said it was well, and that my work in heaven should be the care of the trees growing by the river of life, and that sometimes I could go back to visit my trees on earth, if I wished. That made me very glad, for I knew that so I should see you and our children under the beeches. And while I was wondering whether you would ever know that I was there, the dream dissolved, and I saw the morning light on the tree-tops. What do you think of my dream? Childish, wasn't it?"

She thought a little before she answered.

"It was natural enough, though vague. Of course we could not be buried at the foot of the beech-tree unless Cardinal Mercier would permit a plot of ground to be consecrated there. But come, it is time to go in to breakfast."

She seemed to dismiss the matter from her mind. Yet, as women so often do, she kept all these sayings and pondered them in her heart.

The promise of spring passed into the sultry heat of summer. The storm-cloud of the twentieth century blackened over Europe. The wise men of Berlin made mad by pride, devoted the world not to the Prince of Peace but to the lords of war. In the first week of August the fury of the German invasion broke on Belgium. No one had dared to dream the terrors of that tempest. It was like a return of the Dark Ages. Every home trembled. The pillars of the tranquil house of Azan were shaken.

The daughter was away at school in England, and that was an unmixed blessing. The son was a lieutenant in the Belgian army; and that was right and glorious, but it was also a dreadful anxiety. The father and mother were divided in mind, Whether to stay or take flight with their friends. At last the father decided the hard question.

"It is our duty to stay. We cannot fight for our country, but we can suffer with her. Our daughter is in safety; our son's danger we cannot and would not prevent. How could we really live away from here, our home, our trees? I went to consult the cardinal. He stays, and he advises us to do so. He says that will be the best way to show our devotion. As Christians we must endure the evil that we cannot prevent; but as Belgians our hearts will never consent to it."

That was their attitude as the tide of blood and tears drew nearer to them, surrounded them, swept beyond them, engulfed the whole land. The brutal massacres at Andenne and Dinant were so near that the news arrived before the spilt blood was dry. The exceeding great and bitter cry of anguish came to them from a score of neighboring villages, from a hundred lonely farmhouses. The old botanist withered and faded daily; his wife grew pale and gray. Yet they walked their *via crucis* together, and kept their chosen course.

They fed the hungry and clothed the naked, helped the fugitives and consoled the broken-hearted. They counselled their poor neighbors to good order, and dissuaded the ignorant from the folly and peril of violence. Toward the invading soldiery their conduct was beyond reproach. With no false professions of friendship, they fulfilled the hard services which were required of them. Their servants had been helped away at the beginning of the trouble—all except the old forester and his wife, who refused to leave. With their aid the house was kept open and many of the conquerors lodged there and in the outbuildings. So good were the quarters that a departing Saxon chalked on the gate-post the dubious inscription: *"Gute Leute-nicht auspliin-dern."* Thus the captives at the Chateau d'Azan had a good name even among their enemies. The baron received a military pass which enabled him to move quite freely about the district on his errands of necessity and mercy, and the chateau became a favorite billet for high-born officers.

In the second year of the war an evil chance brought two uninvited guests of very high standing indeed—that is to say in the social ring of Potsdam. Their names are well known. Let us call them Prince Barenberg and Count Ludra. The first was a major, the second a captain. Their value as warriors in the field had not proved equal to their prominence as noblemen, so they were given duty in the rear.

They were vicious coxcombs of the first order. Their uniforms incased them tightly. Like wasps they bent only at the waist. Their flat-topped caps were worn with an aggressive slant, their swords jingled menacingly, their hay-colored mustaches spoke arrogance in every upturned hair. When they bowed it was a mockery; when they smiled it was a sneer. For the comfortable quarters of the Chateau d'Azan they had a gross appreciation, for the enforced hospitality of its owners an insolent condescension. They took it as their due, and resented the silent protest underneath it.

"Excellent wine, Herr Baron," said the prince, who, like his comrade, drank profusely of the best in the cellar. "Your Rudesheimer Berg '94 is *kolossal*. Very friendly of you to save it for us. We Germans know good wine. What?"

"You have that reputation," answered the baron.

"And say," added the count, "let us have a couple of bottles more, dear landlord. You can put it in the bill."

"I shall do so," said the baron gravely. "It shall be put in the bill with other things."

"But why," drawled the prince, "does *la Baronne* never favor us with her company? Still very attractive—musical probably—here is a piano—want good German music—console homesickness."

"Madame is indisposed," answered the baron quietly, "but you may be sure she regrets your absence from home."

The officers looked at each other with half-tipsy, half-angry eyes. They suspected a jest at their expense, but could not quite catch it.

"Impudence," muttered the count, who was the sharper of the two when sober.

"No," said the prince, "it is only stupidity. These Walloons have no wit."

"Come," he added, turning to the baron, "we sing you a good song of fatherland—show how *gemuthlich* we Germans are. You Belgians have no word for that. What?"

He sat down to the piano and pounded out *"Deutschland ueber Alles,"* singing the air in a raucous voice, while Ludra added a rumbling bass.

"What do you think of that? All Germans can sing. *Gemuthlich*. What?"

"You are right," said the baron, with downcast eyes. "We Belgians have no word for that. It is inexpressible—except in German. I bid you good night."

For nearly a fortnight this condition of affairs continued. The baron endured it as best he could, obeying scrupulously the military regulations which necessity laid upon him, and taking his revenge only in long thoughts and words of polite sarcasm which he knew would not be understood. The baroness worked hard at the housekeeping, often cooking and cleaning with her own hands, and rejoicing secretly with her husband over the rare news that came from their daughter in England, from their boy at the front in West Flanders. Sometimes, when the coast was clear, husband and wife walked together under the beech-trees and talked in low tones of the time when the ravenous beast should no more go up on the land.

The two noble officers performed their routine duties, found such amusement as they could in neighboring villages and towns, drank deep at night, and taxed their ingenuity to invent small ways of annoying their hosts, for whom they felt the contemptuous dislike of the injurer for the injured. They were careful, however, to keep their malice within certain bounds, for they knew that the baron was in favor with the commandant of the district.

One morning the baron and his wife, looking from their window in a wing of the house, saw with surprise and horror a score or more of German soldiers assembled beside the beech-avenue, with axes and saws, preparing to begin work.

"What are they going to do there?" cried he in dismay, and hurried down to the dining-room, where the officers sat at breakfast, giving orders to an attentive corporal.

"A thousand pardons, Highness," interrupted the baron; "forgive my haste. But surely you are not going to cut down my avenue of beeches?"

"Why not?" said the prince, swinging around in his chair. "They are good wood."

"But, sir," stammered the baron, trembling with excitement, "those trees—they are an ancient heritage of the house—planted by my grandfather a century ago—an old possession—spare them for their age."

"You exaggerate," sneered the prince. "They are not old. I have on my hunting estate in Thuringia oaks five hundred years old. These trees of yours are mere upstarts. Why shouldn't they be cut? What?"

"But they are very dear to us," pleaded the baron earnestly. "We all love them, my wife and children and I. To us they are sacred. It would be harsh to take them from us."

"Baron," said the prince, with suave malice, "you miss the point. We Germans are never harsh. But we are practical. My soldiers need exercise. The camps need wood. Do you see? What?"

"Certainly," answered the poor baron, humbling himself in his devotion to his trees. "Your Highness makes the point perfectly clear—the need of exercise and wood. But there is plenty of good timber in the forest and the park—much easier to cut. Cannot your men get their wood and their exercise there, and spare my dearest trees?"

Ludra laughed unpleasantly.

"You do not yet understand us, dear landlord. We Germans are a hard-working people, not like the lazy Belgians. The harder the work the better we like it. The soldiers will have a fine time chopping down your tough beeches."

The slender old man drew himself up, his eyes flashed, he was driven to bay.

"You shall not do this," he cried. "It is an outrage, a sacrilege. I shall appeal to the commandant. He will protect my rights."

The officers looked at each other. Deaf to pity, they had keen ears for danger. A reproof, perhaps a punishment from their superior would be most unpleasant. They hesitated to face it. But they were too obstinate to give up their malicious design altogether with a good grace.

"Military necessity," growled the prince, "knows no private rights. I advise you, baron, not to appeal to the commandant. It will be useless, perhaps harmful."

"Here, you," he said gruffly, turning to the corporal, "carry out my orders. Cut the two marked beeches by the gate. Then take your men into the park and cut the biggest trees there. Report for further orders to-morrow morning."

The wooden-faced giant saluted, swung on his heels, and marched stiffly out. The baron followed him quickly.

He knew that entreaties would be wasted on the corporal. How to get to the commandant, that was the question? He would not be allowed to use the telephone which was in the dining-room, nor the automobile which belonged to the officers; nor one of their horses which were in his stable. The only other beast left there was a small and very antique donkey which the children used to drive. In a dilapidated go-cart, drawn by this pattering nag, the baron made such haste as he could along twelve miles of stony road to the district headquarters. There he told his story simply to the commandant and begged protection for his beloved trees.

The old general was of a different type from the fire-eating dandies who played the master at Azan. He listened courteously and gravely. There was a picture in his mind of the old timbered house in the Hohe Venn, where he had spent four years in retirement before the war called him back to the colors. He thought of the tall lindens and the spreading chestnuts around it and imagined how he should feel if he saw them falling under the axe.

Then he said to his petitioner:

"You have acted quite correctly, *Monsieur le Baron*, in bringing this matter quietly to my attention. There is no military necessity for the destruction of your fine trees. I shall put a stop to it at once."

He called his aide-de-camp and gave some instructions in a low tone of voice. When the aide came back from the telephone and reported, the general frowned.

"It is unheard of," he muttered, half to himself, "the way those titled young fools go beyond their orders."

Then he turned to his visitor.

"I am very sorry, *Monsieur le Baron*, but two of your beeches have already fallen. It cannot be helped now. But there shall be no more of it, I promise you. Those young officers are—they are—let us call them overzealous. I will transfer them to another post to-morrow. The German command appreciates the correct conduct of you and *Madame la Baronne.* Is there anything more that I can do for you?"

"I thank your Excellency sincerely," replied the baron. Then he hesitated a moment, as if to weigh his words. "No, *Herr General,* I believe there is nothing more—in which you can help me."

The old soldier's eyelids flickered for an instant. "Then I bid you a very good day," he said, bowing.

The baron hurried home, to share the big good news with his wife. The little bad news she knew already. Together they grieved over the two fallen trees and rejoiced under the golden shadow of their untouched companions. The officers had called for wine, and more wine, and yet more wine, and were drinking deep and singing loud in the dining-room.

In the morning came an orderly with a despatch from headquarters, ordering the prince and the count to duty in a dirty village of the coal region. Their baggage was packed into the automobile, and they mounted their horses and went away in a rage.

"You will be sorry for this, dumbhead," growled the prince, scowling fiercely. "Yes," added Ludra, with a hateful grin, "we shall meet again, dear landlord, and you will be sorry."

Their host bowed and said nothing.

Some weeks later the princely automobile came to the door of the chateau. The forester brought up word that the Prince Barenberg and the Count Ludra were below with a message from headquarters; the commandant wished the baron to come there immediately; the automobile was sent to bring him. He made ready to go. His wife and his servant tried hard to dissuade him: it was late, almost dark, and very cold—not likely the commandant had sent for him—it might be all a trick of those officers—they were hateful men—they would play some cruel prank for revenge. But the old man was obstinate in his resolve; he must do what was required of him, he must not even run the risk of slighting the commandant's wishes; after all, no great harm could come to him.

When he reached the steps he saw the count in the front seat, beside the chauffeur, grinning; and the prince's harsh voice, made soft as possible, called from the shadowy interior of the car:

"Come in, baron. The general has sent for you in a hurry. We will take you like lightning. How fine your beeches look against the sky. What?"

The old man stepped into the dusky car. It rolled down the long aisle, between the smooth gray columns, beneath the fan-tracery of the low arches, out on to the stony highway. Thus the tree-lover was taken from his sanctuary.

He did not return the next day, nor the day after. His wife, tortured by anxiety, went to the district headquarters. The commandant was away. The aide could not enlighten her. There had been no message sent to the baron—that was certain. Major Barenberg and Captain Ludra had been transferred to another command. Unfortunately, nothing could be done except to report the case.

The brave woman was not broken by her anguish, but raised to the height of heroic devotion. She dedicated herself to the search for her husband. The faithful forester, convinced that his master had been killed, was like a slow, sure bloodhound on the track of the murderers. He got a trace of them in a neighboring village, where their car had been seen to pass at dusk on the fatal day. The officers were in it, but not the baron. The forester got a stronger scent of them in a wine-house, where their chauffeur had babbled mysteriously on the following day. The old woodsman followed the trail with inexhaustible patience.

"I shall bring the master's body home," he said to his mistress, "and God will use me to avenge his murder."

A few weeks later he found his master's corpse hidden in a hollow on the edge of the forest, half-covered with broken branches, rotting leaves, and melting snow. There were three bullets in the body. They had been fired at close range.

The widow's heart, passing from the torture of uncertainty to the calm of settled grief, had still a sacred duty to live for. She had not forgotten her husband's dream. She went to the cardinal-archbishop to beg the consecration of a little burial-plot at the foot of the greatest of the beeches of Azan. That wise and brave prince of the church consented with words of tender consolation, and promised his aid in the pursuit of the criminals.

"Eminence," she said, weeping, "you are very good to me. God will reward you. He is just. He will repay. But my heart's desire is to follow my husband's dream."

So the body of the old botanist was brought back to the shadow of the great beech-trees, and was buried there, like the bones of a martyr, within the sanctuary.

Is this the end of the story?

Who can say?

It is written also, among the records of Belgium, that the faithful forester disappeared mysteriously a few weeks later. His body was found in the forest and laid near his master.

Another record tells of the trial of Prince Barenberg and Count Ludra before a court martial, The count was sentenced to ten years of labor *on his own estate*. The death-sentence of the prince was commuted to imprisonment *in some unnamed place*. So far the story of German justice.

But of the other kind of justice—the poetic, the Divine—the record is not yet complete.

I know only that there is a fatherless girl working and praying in a hospital in England, and a fatherless boy fighting and praying in the muddy trenches near Ypres, and a lonely woman walking and praying under certain great beech-trees at the Chateau d'Azan. The burden of their prayer is the same. Night and day it rises to Him who will judge the world in righteousness and before whose eyes the wicked shall not stand.

September, 1918.

THE KING'S HIGH WAY

In the last remnant of Belgium, a corner yet unconquered by the German horde, I saw a tall young man walking among the dunes, between the sodden lowland and the tumbling sea.

The hills where he trod were of sand heaped high by the western winds; and the growth over them was wire-grass and thistles, bayberry and golden broom and stunted pine, with many humble wild flowers—things of no use, yet beautiful.

The sky above was gray; the northern sea was gray; the southern fields were hazy gray over green; the smoke of shells bursting in the air was gray. Gray was the skeleton of the ruined city in the distance; gray were the shattered spires and walls of a dozen hamlets on the horizon; gray, the eyes of the young man who walked in faded blue uniform, in the remnant of Belgium. But there was an indomitable light in his eyes, by which I knew that he was a King.

"Sir," I said, "I am sure that you are his Majesty, the King of Belgium."

He bowed, and a pleasant smile relaxed his tired face.

"Pardon, monsieur," he answered, "but you make the usual mistake in my title. If I were only 'the King of Belgium,' you see, I should have but a poor kingdom now—only this narrow strip of earth, perhaps four hundred square miles of debris, just a *'pou sto,"* a place to stand, enough to fight on, and if need be to die in."

His hand swept around the half-circle of dull landscape visible southward from the top of the loftiest dune, the *Hooge Blikker*. It was a land of slow-winding streams and straight canals and flat fields, with here and there a clump of woods or a slight rise of ground, but for the most part level and monotonous, a checker-board landscape—stretching away until the eyes rested on the low hills beyond Ypres. Now all the placid charm of Flemish fertility as gone from the land—it was scarred and marred and pitted. The shells and mines had torn holes in it; the trenches and barbed-wire entanglements spread over it like a network of scars and welts; the trees were smashed into kindling-wood; the farmhouses were heaps of charred bricks; the shattered villages were like mouths full of broken teeth. As the King looked round at all this, his face darkened and the slight droop of his shoulders grew more marked.

"But, no," he said, turning to me again, "that is not my kingdom. My real title, monsieur, is *King of the Belgians*. It was for their honor, for their liberty, that I was willing to lose my land and risk my crown. While they live and hold true, I stand fast."

Then ran swiftly through me the thought, of how the little Belgian army had fought, how the Belgian people had suffered, rather than surrender the independence of their country to the barbarians. The German cannonade was roaring along the Yser a few miles away; the air trembled with the overload of sound; but between the peals of thunder I could hear the brave song of the skylark climbing his silver stairway of music, undismayed, hopeful, unconquerable. I remembered how the word of this quiet man beside whom I stood had been the inspiration and encouragement of his people through the fierce conflict, the long agony: *"I have faith in our destiny; a nation which defends itself does not perish; God will be with us in that just cause."*

"Sir," I said, "you have a glorious kingdom which shall never be taken away. But as for your land, the fates have been against you. How will you ever get back to it? The Germans are strong as iron and they bar the way. Will you make a peace with them and take what they have so often offered you?"

"Never," he answered calmly; "that is not the way home, it is the way to dishonor. When God brings me back, my army and my Queen are going with me to liberate our people. There is only one way that leads there—the King's high way. Look, *monsieur,* you can see the beginning of it down there. I hope you wish me well on that road, for I shall never take another."

So he bade me good afternoon very courteously and walked away among the dunes to his little cottage at La Panne.

Looking down through the light haze of evening I saw a strip of the straight white road leading eastward across the level land. At the beginning of it there was a broken bridge; in places it seemed torn up by shells; it disappeared in the violet dusk. But as I looked a vision came.

The bridge is restored, the road mended and built up, and on that highway rides the King in his faded uniform with the Queen in white beside him. At their approach ruined villages rejoice aloud and ancient towns break forth into singing.

In Bruges the royal comrades stand beside the gigantic monument in the centre of the Great Market, and above the shouting of the multitude the music of the old belfry floats unheard. Ghent and Antwerp have put on their glad raiment, and in their crooked streets and crowded squares joy flows like a river surging as it goes. Into Brussels I see this man and woman ride through a welcome that rises around them like the voice of many waters— the welcome of those who have waited and suffered, the welcome of those to whom liberty and honor were more dear than life. In the *Grande Place,* the antique, carven, gabled houses are gay with fluttering banners; the people delivered from the cruel invader sing lustily the *Marseillaise* and the old songs of Belgium.

In the midst, Albert and Elizabeth sit quietly upon their horses. They have come home. Not by the low road of cowardly surrender; not by the crooked road of compromise and falsehood; not by the soft road of ease and self-indulgence; but by the straight road of faith and courage and self-sacrifice—the King's High Way.

HALF-TOLD TALES

THE TRAITOR IN THE HOUSE

The Guest, who came from beyond the lake, had lived in the house for years and had the freedom of it, so that he had become quite like a member of the family. He was friendly treated and well lodged. Indeed, some thought he had the best room of all, for though it was in the wing, it was spacious and well warmed, and had a side door, so that he could go in and out freely by day or night.

It must be said that he had earned his living on the place, being industrious and useful, a very handy man about the house; and the children had a liking for him because he sang merry songs and told beautiful fairy-tales.

So he was all the more surprised and aggrieved when the Master of the house said to him one night, as they sat late by the fire:

"I suspect you."

"But of what?" cried the Guest.

"Of caring more for the house that you came from than for the house that you live in."

"But you know I was at home there once," said the Guest, "would you have me forget that? Surely you will not deny me the freedom of my thoughts and memories and fond feelings. Would you make me less than a man?"

"No," said the Master, "but I will ask you to choose between your old home and your new home now. The house in which you lived formerly is become our enemy—a nest of brigands and bloody men. They have killed a child of ours on the highway. They threaten us to-night with an attack in force. Tell me plainly where you stand."

The Guest looked down his nose toward the smouldering embers of the fire. He knocked out the dottle of his pipe on one of the andirons. Two fat tears rolled down his cheeks; he was very sentimental.

"I am with you," he said.

"Good," said the Master, "now let us make the house fast!" {Illustration with caption: 'I will ask you to choose between your old home and your new home now.'}

So they closed and barred the shutters and locked and bolted the front door.

Then they lighted their bedroom candles and bade each other good night.

But as the Guest went along his dim corridor, the Master turned and followed him very softly on tiptoe, watching.

Outside the house, in the darkness, there was a sound of many shuffling feet and whispering voices.

When the Guest came to the side door he tried the latch, to see that it was working freely. He moved the bolt, not forward into its socket, but backward so that it should be no hindrance. In the window beside the doorway he set his candle. So the house was ready for late-comers.

Then the Guest sighed a little. "They are my old friends," he murmured, "my dear old friends! I could not leave them out in the cold. I am not responsible for what they do. Only I must my old affection prove." So he sighed again and turned softly to his bed.

But as he turned the Master stood before him and took him by the throat.

"Traitor!" he cried. "You would betray the innocent. Already your soul is stained with my sleeping children's blood." And with his hands he choked the false Guest to death.

Then he shot the bolt of the side door, and barred the window, and called the servants, and made ready to defend the house.

Great was the fighting that night. In the morning, when the robbers were driven off, the false Guest was buried, outside the garden, in an unmarked grave.

February 2, 1918.

JUSTICE OF THE ELEMENTS

So the Criminal with a Crown came to the end of his resources. He had told his last lie, but not even his servants would believe it. He had made his last threat, but no living soul feared it. He had put forth his last stroke of violence and cruelty, but it fell short.

When he saw his own image reflected in the eyes of men, and knew what he had done to the world and what had come of his evil design, he was afraid, and cried, "Let the Earth swallow me!" And the Earth opened, and swallowed him.

But so great was the harm that he had wrought upon the Earth, and so deeply had he drenched it with blood, that it could not contain him. So the Earth opened again, and spewed him forth.

Then he cried, "Let the Sea hide me!" And the waves rolled over his head.

But the Sea, whereon he had wrought iniquity, and filled the depths thereof with the bones of the innocent, could not endure him and threw him up on the shore as refuse.

Then he cried, "Let the Air carry me away!" And the strong winds blew, and lifted him up so that he felt exalted.

But the pure Air, wherein he had let loose the vultures of hate, dropping death upon helpless women and harmless babes, found the burden and the stench of him intolerable, and let him fall.

And as he was falling he cried, "Let the Fire give me a refuge!" So the Fire, wherewith he had consumed the homes of men, rejoiced; and the flames which he had compelled to do his will in wickedness leaped up as he drew near.

"Welcome, old master!" roared the Fire. "Be my slave!"

Then he perceived that there was no hope for him in the justice of the elements. And he said, "I will seek mercy of Him against whom I have most offended."

So he fled to the foot of the Great White Throne. And as he kneeled there, broken and abased, the world was silent, waiting for the sentence of the Judge of All.

August, 1918.

ASHES OF VENGEANCE

Dun was a hard little city, proud and harsh; but impregnable because it was built upon a high rock. The host of the Visigoths had besieged it for months in vain. Then came a fugitive from the city, at midnight, to the tent of Alaric, the Chief of the besiegers.

The man was haggard and torn. His eyes were wild, his hands trembling. The Chief held and steadied him with a look.

"Who are you?" he asked. "Your name, the purpose that brings you here?"

"My name," said the man, "is the Avenger. For thirty years I have lived in Dun, and the people have been unjust and cruel to me. They persecuted my family, because they hated me. My wife died of a broken heart, my children of starvation. I have just escaped from the prison of Dun, and come to tell you how the city may be taken. There is a secret pathway, a hidden entrance. I know it and can reveal it to you."

"Good," said the Chief, measuring the man with tranquil eyes, "but what is your price?"

"Vengeance," said the man, "I ask only the right to revenge my sufferings upon those who have inflicted them, when you have taken the city."

Alaric bent his head and was silent for a moment. "It is a fair price," he said, "and I will pay it. Tell me the way to take the city, and I will leave at your command a troop of soldiers sufficient to work your will on it afterward."

II

The trumpet sounded the capture of the city in the morning. The Avenger, waking late from his troubled sleep, led his soldiers through the open gate.

It was like a city of the dead, and the bodies of those who had been killed in the last defense, lay where they had fallen. Empty and silent were the streets where lie had so often walked in humiliation. Gone were the familiar faces that had frowned on him and mocked him. The houses at whose doors he had often knocked were vacant. His wrath sank within him, and the arrow of solitude pierced him to the heart.

Then he came to the belfry, and there was the bell-ringer, one of the worst of his ancient persecutors, standing at the entrance of the tower.

"Why are you here?" said the Avenger.

"By the orders of King Alaric," answered the bell-ringer, "to ring the bells when peace comes to the city."

"Ring now," said the Avenger, "ring now!"

Then, at the sound of the bells, the people who had concealed themselves at Alaric's command came trooping forth from the cellars and caves where they had been hiding,—old men and women and children, a motley throng of sufferers.

The Avenger looked at them and the tears ran down his cheeks, because he remembered.

"Listen," he said, "don't be afraid. These soldiers are going on to join their army. You have done me great wrong. But the fire of hatred is burnt out, and in the ashes of vengeance we are going to plant the seeds of peace."

December, 1918.

THE BROKEN SOLDIER AND THE MAID OF FRANCE

THE UNSPOKEN SOLDIER AND THE
MAID OF FRANCE

I. THE MEETING AT THE SPRING

Along the old Roman road that crosses the rolling hills from the upper waters of the Marne to the Meuse a soldier of France was passing in the night.

In the broader pools of summer moonlight he showed as a hale and husky fellow of about thirty years, with dark hair and eyes and a handsome, downcast face. His uniform was faded and dusty; not a trace of the horizon blue was left, only a gray shadow. He had no knapsack on his back, no gun on his shoulder. Wearily and doggedly he plodded his way, without eyes for the veiled beauty of the sleeping country. The quick, firm military step was gone. He trudged like a tramp, choosing always the darker side of the road.

He was a figure of flight, a broken soldier.

Presently the road led him into a thick forest of oaks and beeches, and so to the crest of a hill overlooking a long open valley with wooded heights beyond. Below him was the pointed spire of some temple or shrine, lying at the edge of the wood, with no houses near it. Farther down he could see a cluster of white houses with the tower of a church in the centre. Other villages were dimly visible up and down the valley on either slope. The cattle were lowing from the barnyards. The cocks crowed for the dawn. Already the moon had sunk behind the western trees. But the valley was still bathed in its misty, vanishing light. Over the eastern ridge the gray glimmer of the little day was rising, faintly tinged with rose. It was time for the broken soldier to seek his covert and rest till night returned.

So he stepped aside from the road and found a little dell thick with underwoods, and in it a clear spring gurgling among the ferns and mosses. Around the opening grew wild gooseberries and golden broom and a few tall spires of purple foxglove. He drew off his dusty boots and socks and bathed his feet in a small pool, drying them with fern leaves. Then he took a slice of bread and a piece of cheese from his pocket and made his breakfast. Going to the edge of the thicket, he parted the branches and peered out over the vale.

Its eaves sloped gently to the level floor where the river loitered in loops and curves. The sun was just topping the eastern hills; the heads of the trees were dark against a primrose sky.

In the fields the hay had been cut and gathered. The aftermath was already greening the moist places. Cattle and sheep sauntered out to pasture. A thin silvery mist floated here and there, spreading in broad sheets over the wet ground and shredding into filmy scarves and ribbons as the breeze caught it among the pollard willows and poplars on the border of the stream. Far away the water glittered where the river made a sudden bend or a long smooth reach. It was like the flashing of distant shields. Overhead a few white clouds climbed up from the north. The rolling ridges, one after another, enfolded the valley as far as eye could see; dark green set in pale green, with here and there an arm of forest running down on a sharp promontory to meet and turn the meandering stream.

"It must be the valley of the Meuse," said the soldier. "My faith, but France is beautiful and tranquil here!"

The northerly wind was rising. The clouds climbed more swiftly. The poplars shimmered, the willows glistened, the veils of mist vanished. From very far away there came a rumbling thunder, heavy, insistent, continuous, punctuated with louder crashes.

"It is the guns," muttered the soldier, shivering. "It is the guns around Verdun! Those damned Boches!"

He turned back into the thicket and dropped among the ferns beside the spring. Stretching himself with a gesture of abandon, he pillowed his face on his crossed arms to sleep.

A rustling in the bushes roused him. He sprang to his feet quickly. It was a priest, clad in a dusty cassock, his long black beard streaked with gray. He came slowly treading up beside the trickling rivulet, carrying a bag on a stick over his shoulder.

"Good morning, my son," he said. "You have chosen a pleasant spot to rest."

The soldier, startled, but not forgetting his manners learned from boyhood, stood up and lifted his hand to take off his cap. It was already lying on the ground. "Good morning, Father," he answered, "I did not choose the place, but stumbled on it by chance. It is pleasant enough, for I am very tired and have need of sleep."

"No doubt," said the priest. "I can see that you look weary, and I beg you to pardon me if I have interrupted your repose. But why do you say you came here 'by chance'? If you are a good Christian you know that nothing is by chance. All is ordered and designed by Providence."

"So they told me in church long ago," said the soldier coldly; "but now it does not seem so true—at least not with me."

The first feeling of friendliness and respect into which he had been surprised was passing. He had fallen back into the mood of his journey—mistrust, secrecy, resentment.

The priest caught the tone. His gray eyes under their bushy brows looked kindly but searchingly at the soldier and smiled a little. He set down his bag and leaned on his stick. "Well," he said, "I can tell you one thing, my son. At all events it was not chance that brought me here. I came with a purpose."

The soldier started a little, stung by suspicion. "What then," he cried, roughly, "were you looking for me? What do you know of me? What is this talk of chance and purpose?"

"Come, come," said the priest, his smile spreading from his eyes to his lips, "do not be angry. I assure you that I know nothing of you whatever, not even your name nor why you are here. When I said that I came with a purpose I meant only that a certain thought, a wish, led me to this spot. Let us sit together awhile beside the spring and make better acquaintance."

"I do not desire it," said the soldier, with a frown.

"But you will not refuse it?" queried the priest gently. "It is not good to refuse the request of one old enough to be your father. Look, I have here some excellent tobacco and cigarette-papers. Let us sit down and smoke together. I will tell you who I am and the purpose that brought me here."

The soldier yielded grudgingly, not knowing what else to do. They sat down on a mossy bank beside the spring, and while the blue smoke of their cigarettes went drifting under the little trees the priest began:

"My name is Antoine Courcy. I am the cure of Darney, a village among the Reaping Hook Hills, a few leagues south from here. For twenty-five years I have reaped the harvest of heaven in that blessed little field. I am sorry to leave it. But now this war, this great battle for freedom and the life of France, calls me. It is a divine vocation. France has need of all her sons to-day, even the old ones. I cannot keep the love of God in my heart unless I follow the love of country in my life. My younger brother, who used to be the priest of the next parish to mine, was in the army. He has fallen. I am going to replace him. I am on my way to join the troops—as a chaplain, if they will; if not, then as a private. I must get into the army of France or be left out of the host of heaven."

The soldier had turned his face away and was plucking the lobes from a frond of fern. "A brave resolve, Father," he said, with an ironic note. "But you have not yet told me what brings you off your road, to this place."

"I will tell you," replied the priest eagerly; "it is the love of Jeanne d'Arc, the Maid who saved France long ago. You know about her?"

"A little," nodded the soldier. "I have learned in the school. She was a famous saint."

"Not yet a saint," said the priest earnestly; "the Pope has not yet pronounced her a saint. But it will be done soon. Already he has declared her among the

Blessed Ones. To me she is the most blessed of all. She never thought of herself or of a saint's crown. She gave her life entire for France. And this is the place that she came from! Think of that—right here!"

"I did not know that," said the soldier.

"But yes," the priest went on, kindling. "I tell you it was here that the Maid of France received her visions and set out to her work. You see that village below us—look out through the branches—that is Domremy, where she was born. That spire just at the edge of the wood—you saw that? It is the basilica they have built to her memory. It is full of pictures of her. It stands where the old beech-tree, 'Fair May,' used to grow. There she heard the voices and saw the saints who sent her on her mission. And this is the Gooseberry Spring, the Well of the Good Fairies. Here she came with the other children, at the festival of the well-dressing, to spread their garlands around it, and sing, and eat their supper on the green. Heavenly voices spoke to her, but the others did not hear them. Often did she drink of this water. It became a fountain of life springing up in her heart. I have come to drink at the same source. It will strengthen me as a sacrament. Come, son, let us take it together as we go to our duty in battle!"

Father Courcy stood up and opened his old black bag. He took out a small metal cup. He filled it carefully at the spring. He made the sign of the cross over it.

"In the name of the Father, the Son, and the Holy Spirit," he murmured, "blessed and holy is this water." Then he held the cup toward the soldier. "Come, let us share it and make our vows together."

The bright drops trembled and fell from the bottom of the cup. The soldier sat still, his head in his hands.

"No," he answered heavily, "I cannot take it. I am not worthy. Can a man take a sacrament without confessing his sins?"

Father Courcy looked at him with pitying eyes. "I see," he said slowly; "I see, my son. You have a burden on your heart. Well, I will stay with you and try to lift it. But first I shall make my own vow."

He raised the cup toward the sky. A tiny brown wren sang canticles of rapture in the thicket. A great light came into the priest's face—a sun-ray from the east, far beyond the treetops.

"Blessed Jeanne d'Arc, I drink from thy fountain in thy name. I vow my life to thy cause. Aid me, aid this my son, to fight valiantly for freedom and for France. In the name of God, Amen."

The soldier looked up at him. Wonder, admiration, and shame were struggling in the look. Father Courcy wiped the empty cup carefully and put it back in his bag. Then he sat down beside the soldier, laying a fatherly hand on his shoulder.

"Now, my son, you shall tell me what is on your heart."

II. THE GREEN CONFESSIONAL

For a long time the soldier remained silent. His head was bowed. His shoulders drooped. His hands trembled between his knees. He was wrestling with himself.

"No," he cried, at last, "I cannot, I dare not tell you. Unless, perhaps"—his voice faltered—"you could receive it under the seal of confession? But no. How could you do that? Here in the green woods? In the open air, beside a spring? Here is no confessional."

"Why not?" asked Father Courcy. "It is a good place, a holy place. Heaven is over our heads and very near. I will receive your confession here."

The soldier knelt among the flowers. The priest pronounced the sacred words. The soldier began his confession:

"I, Pierre Duval, a great sinner, confess my fault, my most grievous fault, and pray for pardon." He stopped for a moment and then continued, "But first I must tell you, Father, just who I am and where I come from and what brings me here."

"Go on, Pierre Duval, go on. That is what I am waiting to hear. Be simple and very frank."

"Well, then, I am from the parish of Laucourt, in the pleasant country of the Barrois not far from Bar-sur-Aube. My word, but that is a pretty land, full of orchards and berry-gardens! Our old farm there is one of the prettiest and one of the best, though it is small. It was hard to leave it when the call to the colors came, two years ago. But I was glad to go. My heart was high and strong for France. I was in the Nth Infantry, We were in the centre division under General Foch at the battle of the Marne. *Fichtre!* but that was fierce fighting! And what a general! He did not know how to spell 'defeat.' He wrote it 'victory.' Four times we went across that cursed Marsh of St.-Gond. The dried mud was trampled full of dead bodies. The trickling streams of water ran red. Four times we were thrown back by the boches. You would have thought that was enough. But the general did not think so. We went over again on the fifth day, and that time we stayed. The Germans could not stand against us. They broke and ran. The roads where we chased them were full of empty wine-bottles. In one village we caught three officers and a dozen men dead drunk. *Bigre!* what a fine joke!"

Pierre, leaning back upon his heels, was losing himself in his recital. His face lighted up, his hands were waving. Father Courcy bent forward with shining eyes.

"Continue," he cried. "This is a beautiful confession—no sin yet. Continue, Pierre."

"Well, then, after that we were fighting here and there, on the Aisne, on the Ailette, everywhere. Always the same story—Germans rolling down on us in flood, green-gray waves. But the foam on them was fire and steel. The shells of the barrage swept us like hailstones. We waited, waited in our trenches, till the green-gray mob was near enough. Then the word came. *Sapristi!* We let loose with mitrailleuse, rifle, field-gun, everything that would throw death. It did not seem like fighting with men. It was like trying to stop a monstrous thing, a huge, terrible mass that was rushing on to overwhelm us. The waves tumbled and broke before they reached us. Sometimes they fell flat. Sometimes they turned and rushed the other way. It was wild, wild, like a change of the wind and tide in a storm, everything torn and confused. Then perhaps the word came to go over the top and at them. That was furious. That was fighting with men, for sure—bayonet, revolver, rifle-butt, knife, anything that would kill. Often I sickened at the blood and the horror of it. But something inside of me shouted: 'Fight on! It is for France. It is for "L'Alouette" thy farm; for thy wife, thy little ones. Will you let them be ruined by those beasts of Germans? What are they doing here on French soil? Brigands, butchers, apaches! Drive them out; and if they will not go, kill them so they can do no more shameful deeds. Fight on!' So I killed all I could."

The priest nodded his head grimly. "You were right, Pierre; your voice spoke true. It was a dreadful duty that you were doing. The Gospel tells us if we are smitten on one cheek we must turn the other. But it does not tell us to turn the cheek of a little child, of the woman we love, the country we belong to. No! that would be disgraceful, wicked, un-Christian. It would be to betray the innocent! Continue, my son."

"Well, then," Pierre went on, his voice deepening and his face growing more tense, "then we were sent to Verdun. That was the hottest place of all. It was at the top of the big German drive. The whole sea rushed and fell on us— big guns, little guns, poison-gas, hand-grenades, liquid fire, bayonets, knives, and trench-clubs. Fort after fort went down. The whole pack of hell was loose and raging. I thought of that crazy, chinless Crown Prince sitting in his safe little cottage hidden in the woods somewhere—they say he had flowers and vines planted around it—drinking stolen champagne and sicking on his dogs of death. He was in no danger. I cursed him in my heart, that blood-lord! The shells rained on Verdun. The houses were riddled; the cathedral was pierced in a dozen places; a hundred fires broke out. The old citadel held good. The outer forts to the north and east were taken. Only the last ring was left. We common soldiers did not know much about what was happening. The big battle was beyond our horizon. But that General Petain, he knew it all. Ah, that is a wise man, I can tell you! He sent us to this place or that place where the defense was most needed. We went gladly, without fear or holding back. We were resolute that those mad dogs should not get through. *'They shall not pass'!* And they did not pass!"

"Glorious!" cried the priest, drinking the story in. "And you, Pierre? Where were you, what were you doing?"

"I was at Douaumont, that fort on the highest hill of all. The Germans took it. It cost them ten thousand men. The ground around it was like a wood-yard piled with logs. The big shell-holes were full of corpses. There were a few of us that got away. Then our company was sent to hold the third redoubt on the slope in front of Port de Vaux. Perhaps you have heard of that redoubt. That was a bitter job. But we held it many days and nights. The boches pounded us from Douaumont and from the village of Vaux. They sent wave after wave up the slope to drive us out. But we stuck to it. That ravine of La Caillette was a boiling caldron of men. It bubbled over with smoke and fire. Once, when their second wave had broken just in front of us, we went out to hurry the fragments down the hill. Then the guns from Douaumont and the village of Vaux hammered us. Our men fell like ninepins. Our lieutenant called to us to turn back. Just then a shell tore away his right leg at the knee. It hung by the skin and tendons. He was a brave lad. I could not leave him to die there. So I hoisted him on my back. Three shots struck me. They felt just like hard blows from a heavy fist. One of them made my left arm powerless. I sank my teeth in the sleeve of my lieutenant's coat as it hung over my shoulder. I must not let him fall off my back. Somehow—God knows how—I gritted through to our redoubt. They took my lieutenant from my shoulders. And then the light went out."

The priest leaned forward, his hands stretched out around the soldier. "But you are a hero," he cried. "Let me embrace you!"

The soldier drew back, shaking his head sadly. "No," he said, his voice breaking—"no, my Father, you must not embrace me now. I may have been a brave man once. But now I am a coward. Let me tell you everything. My wounds were bad, but not desperate. The *brancardiers* carried me down to Verdun, at night I suppose, but I was unconscious; and so to the hospital at Vaudelaincourt. There were days and nights of blankness mixed with pain. Then I came to my senses and had rest. It was wonderful. I thought that I had died and gone to heaven. Would God it had been so! Then I should have been with my lieutenant. They told me he had passed away in the redoubt. But that hospital was beautiful, so clean and quiet and friendly. Those white nurses were angels. They handled me like a baby. I would have liked to stay there. I had no desire to get better. But I did. One day several officers visited the hospital. They came to my cot, where I was sitting up. The highest of them brought out a Cross of War and pinned it on the breast of my nightshirt. 'There,' he said, 'you are decorated, Pierre Duval! You are one of the heroes of France. You are soon going to be perfectly well and to fight again bravely for your country.' I thanked him, but I knew better. My body might get perfectly well, but something in my soul was broken. It was worn out. The thin spring had snapped. I could never fight again. Any loud noise made me shake all over. I knew that I could never face a battle—impossible! I should certainly lose my nerve and run away. It is a damned feeling, that broken something inside of one. I can't describe it."

Pierre stopped for a moment and moistened his dry lips with the tip of his tongue.

"I know," said Father Courcy. "I understand perfectly what you want to say. It was like being lost and thinking that nothing could save you; a feeling that is piercing and dull at the same time, like a heavy weight pressing on you with sharp stabs in it. It was what they call shell-shock, a terrible thing. Sometimes it drives men crazy for a while. But the doctors know what to do for that malady. It passes. You got over it."

"No," answered Pierre, "the doctors may not have known that I had it. At all events, they did not know what to do for it. It did not pass. It grew worse. But I hid it, talking very little, never telling anybody how I felt. They said I was depressed and needed cheering up. All the while there was that black snake coiled around my heart, squeezing tighter and tighter. But my body grew stronger every day. The wounds were all healed. I was walking around. In July the doctor-in-chief sent for me to his office. He said: 'You are cured, Pierre Duval, but you are not yet fit to fight. You are low in your mind. You need cheering up. You are to have a month's furlough and repose. You shall go home to your farm. How is it that you call it?' I suppose I had been babbling about it in my sleep and one of the nurses had told him. He was always that way, that little Doctor Roselly, taking an interest in the men, talking with them and acting friendly. I said the farm was called 'L'Alouette"—rather a foolish name. 'Not, at all,' he answered; 'it is a fine name, with the song of a bird in it. Well, you are going back to "L'Alouette" to hear the lark sing for a month, to kiss your wife and your children, to pick gooseberries and currants. Eh, my boy, what do you think of that? Then, when the month is over, you will be a new man. You will be ready to fight again at Verdun. Remember they have not passed and they shall not pass! Good luck to you, Pierre Duval.' So I went back to the farm as fast as I could go."

He was silent for a few moments, letting his thoughts wander through the pleasant paths of that little garden of repose. His eyes were dreaming, his lips almost smiled.

"It was sweet at *'L'Alouette,"* very sweet, Father. The farm was in pretty good order and the kitchen-garden was all right, though, the flowers had been a little neglected. You see, my wife, Josephine, she is a very clever woman. She had kept up the things that were the most necessary. She had hired one of the old neighbors and a couple of boys to help her with the ploughing and planting. The harvest she sold as it stood. Our yoke of cream-colored oxen and the roan horse were in good condition. Little Pierrot, who is five, and little Josette, who is three, were as brown as berries. They hugged me almost to death. But it was Josephine herself who was the best of all. She is only twenty-six, Father, and so beautiful still, with her long chestnut hair and her eyes like stones shining under the waters of a brook. I tell you it was good to get her in my arms again and feel her lips on mine. And to wake in the early morning, while the birds were singing, and see her face beside me on the white pillow, sleeping like a child, that was a little bit of Paradise. But I do wrong to tell you of all this, Father."

"Proceed, my big boy," nodded the priest. "You are saying nothing wrong. I was a man before I was a priest. It is all natural, what you are saying, and all according to God's law—no sin in it. Proceed. Did your happiness do you good?" Pierre shook his head doubtfully. The look of dejection came back to his face. He frowned as if something puzzled and hurt him. "Yes and no. That is the strange thing. It made me thankful—that goes without saying. But it did not make me any stronger in my heart. Perhaps it was too sweet. I thought too much of it. I could not bear to think of anything else. The idea of the war was hateful, horrible, disgusting. The noise and the dirt of it, the mud in the autumn and the bitter cold in the winter, the rats and the lice in the dugouts, And then the fury of the charge, and the everlasting killing, killing, or being killed! The danger had seemed little or nothing to me when I was there. But at a distance it was frightful, unendurable. I knew that I could never stand up to it again. Besides, already I had done my share—enough for two or three men. Why must I go back into that hell? It was not fair. Life was too dear to be risking it all the time. I could not endure it. France? France? Of course I love France. But my farm and my life with Josephine and the children mean more to me. The thing that made me a good soldier is broken inside me. It is beyond mending."

His voice sank lower and lower. Father Courcy looked at him gravely.

"But your farm is a part of France. You belong to France. He that saveth his life shall lose it!"

"Yes, yes, I know. But my farm is such a small part of France. I am only one man. What difference does one man make, except to himself? Moreover, I had done my part, that was certain. Twenty times, really, my life had been lost. Why must I throw it away again? Listen, Father. There is a village in the

Vosges, near the Swiss border, where a relative of mine lives. If I could get to him he would take me in and give me some other clothes and help me over the frontier into Switzerland. There I could change my name and find work until the war is over. That was my plan. So I set out on my journey, following the less-travelled roads, tramping by night and sleeping by day. Thus I came to this spring at the same time as you by chance, by pure chance. Do you see?"

Father Courcy looked very stern and seemed about to speak in anger. Then he shook his head, and said quietly: "No, I do not see that at all. It remains to be seen whether it was by chance. But tell me more about your sin. Did you let your wife, Josephine, know what you were going to do? Did you tell her good-by, parting for Switzerland?"

"Why, no! I did not dare. She would never have forgiven me. So I slipped down to the post-office at Bar-sur-Aube and stole a telegraph blank. It was ten days before my furlough was out. I wrote a message to myself calling me back to the colors at once. I showed it to her. Then I said good-by. I wept. She did not cry one tear. Her eyes were stars. She embraced me a dozen times. She lifted up each of the children to hug me. Then she cried: 'Go now, my brave man. Fight well. Drive the damned boches out. It is for us and for France. God protect you. *Au revoir!*' I went down the road silent. I felt like a dog. But I could not help it."

"And you were a dog," said the priest sternly. "That is what you were, and what you remain unless you can learn to help it. You lied to your wife. You forged; you tricked her who trusted you. You have done the thing which you yourself say she would never forgive. If she loves you and prays for you now, you have stolen that love and that prayer. You are a thief. A true daughter of France could never love a coward to-day."

"I know, I know," sobbed Pierre, burying his face in the weeds. "Yet I did it partly for her, and I could not do otherwise."

"Very little for her, and a hundred times for yourself," said the priest indignantly. "Be honest. If there was a little bit of love for her, it was the kind of love she did not want. She would spit upon it. If you are going to Switzerland now you are leaving her forever. You can never go back to Josephine again. You are a deserter. She would cast you out, coward!"

The broken soldier lay very still, almost as if he were dead. Then he rose slowly to his feet, with a pale, set face. He put his hand behind his back and drew out a revolver. "It is true," he said slowly, "I am a coward. But not altogether such a coward as you think, Father. It is not merely death that I fear. I could face that, I think. Here, take this pistol and shoot me now! No one will know. You can say you shot a deserter, or that I attacked you. Shoot me now, Father, and let me out of this trouble."

Father Courcy looked at him with amazement. Then he took the pistol, uncocked it cautiously, and dropped it behind him. He turned to Pierre and regarded him curiously. "Go on with your confession, Pierre. Tell me about this strange kind of cowardice which can face death."

The soldier dropped on his knees again, and went on in a low, shaken voice: "It is this, Father. By my broken soul, this is the very root of it. I am afraid of fear."

The priest thought for an instant. "But that is not reasonable, Pierre. It is nonsense. Fear cannot hurt you. If you fight it you can conquer it. At least you can disregard it, march through it, as if it were not there."

"Not this fear," argued the soldier, with a peasant's obstinacy. "This is something very big and dreadful. It has no shape, but a dead-white face and red, blazing eyes full of hate and scorn. I have seen it in the dark. It is stronger than I am. Since something is broken inside of me, I know I can never conquer it. No, it would wrap its shapeless arms around me and stab me to the heart with its fiery eyes. I should turn and run in the middle of the battle. I should trample on my wounded comrades. I should be shot in the back and die in disgrace. O my God! my God! who can save me from this? It is horrible. I cannot bear it."

The priest laid his hand gently on Pierre's quivering shoulder. "Courage, my son!"

"I have none."

"Then say to yourself that fear is nothing."

"It would be a lie. This fear is real."

"Then cease to tremble at it; kill it."

"Impossible. I am afraid of fear."

"Then carry it as your burden, your cross. Take it back to Verdun with you."

"I dare not. It would poison the others. It would bring me to dishonor."

"Pray to God for help."

"He will not answer me. I am a wicked man. Father, I have made my confession. Will you give me a penance and absolve me?"

"Promise to go back to the army and fight as well as you can."

"Alas! that is what I cannot do. My mind is shaken to pieces. Whither shall I turn? I can decide nothing. I am broken. I repent of my great sin. Father, for the love of God, speak the word of absolution."

Pierre lay on his face, motionless, his arms stretched out. The priest rose and went to the spring. He scooped up a few drops in the hollow of his hand. He sprinkled it like holy water upon the soldier's head. A couple of tears fell with it.

"God have pity on you, my son, and bring you back to yourself. The word of absolution is not for me to speak while you think of forsaking France. Put that thought away from you, do penance for it, and you will be absolved from your great sin."

Pierre turned over and lay looking up at the priest's face and at the blue sky with white cloude drifting across it. He sighed. "Ah, if that could only be! But I have not the strength. It is impossible."

"All things are possible to him that believeth. Strength will come. Perhaps Jeanne d'Arc herself will help you."

"She would never speak to a man like me. She is a great saint, very high in heaven."

"She was a farmer's lass, a peasant like yourself. She would speak to you, gladly and kindly, if you saw her, and in your own language, too. Trust her."

"But I do not know enough about her."

"Listen, Pierre. I have thought for you. I will appoint the first part of your penance. You shall take the risk of being recognized and caught. You shall go down to the village and visit the places that belong to her—her basilica, her house, her church. Then you shall come back here and wait until you know—until you surely know what you must do. Will you promise this?"

Pierre had risen and looked up at the priest with tear-stained face. But his eyes were quieter. "Yes, Father, I can promise you this much faithfully."

"Now I must go my way. Farewell, my son. Peace in war be with you." He held out his hand.

Pierre took it reverently. "And with you, Father," he murmured.

III. THE ABSOLVING DREAM

Antoine Courcy was one of those who are fitted and trained by nature for the cure of souls. If you had spoken to him of psychiatry he would not have understood you. The long word would have been Greek to him. But the thing itself he knew well. The preliminary penance which he laid upon Pierre Duval was remedial. It belonged to the true healing art which works first in the spirit.

When the broken soldier went down the hill, in the blaze of the mid-morning sunlight, toward Domremy, there was much misgiving and confusion in his thoughts. He did not comprehend why he was going, except that he had promised. He was not sure that some one might not know him, or perhaps out of mere curiosity stop him and question him. It was a reluctant journey.

Yet it was in effect an unconscious pilgrimage to the one health-resort that his soul needed. For Domremy and the region round about are saturated with the most beautiful story of France. The life of Jeanne d'Arc, simple and mysterious, humble and glorious, most human and most heavenly, flows under that place like a hidden stream, rising at every turn in springs and fountains. The poor little village lives in and for her memory. Her presence haunts the ridges and the woods, treads the green pastures, follows the white road beside the river, and breathes in the never-resting valley-wind that marries the flowers in June and spreads their seed in August.

At the small basilica built to her memory on the place where her old beech-tree, "Fair May," used to stand, there was an ancient caretaker who explained to Pierre the pictures from the life of the Maid with which the walls are decorated. They are stiff and conventional, but the old man found them wonderful and told with zest the story of *La Pucelle*—how she saw her first vision; how she recognized the Dauphin in his palace at Chinon; how she broke the siege of Orleans; how she saw Charles crowned in the cathedral at Rheims; how she was burned at the stake in Rouen. But they could not kill her soul. She saved France.

In the village church there was a priest from the border of Alsace, also a pilgrim like Pierre, but one who knew the shrine better. He showed the difference between the new and the old parts of the building. Certain things the Maid herself had seen and touched.

"Here is the old holy-water basin, an antique, broken column hollowed out on top. Here her fingers must have rested often. Before this ancient statue of St. Michel she must have often knelt to say her prayers. The cure of the parish was a friend of hers and loved to talk with her. She was a good girl, devout and obedient, not learned, but a holy and great soul. She saved France."

In the house where she was born and passed her childhood a crippled old woman was custodian. It was a humble dwelling of plastered stone standing between two tall fir-trees, with ivy growing over the walls, lilies and hollyhocks blooming in the garden. Pierre found it not half so good a house as *"L'Alouette."* But to the custodian it was more precious than a palace. In this upper room with its low mullioned window the Maid began her life. Here, in the larger room below, is the kneeling statue which the Princess Marie d'Orleans made of her. Here, to the right, under the sloping roof, with its worm-eaten beams, she slept and prayed and worked.

"See, here is the bread-board between two timbers where she cut the bread for the *croute au pot*. From this small window she looked at night and saw the sanctuary light burning in the church. Here, also, as well as in the garden and in the woods, her heavenly voices spoke to her and told her what she must do for her king and her country. She was not afraid or ashamed, though she lived in so small a house. Here in this very room she braided her hair and put on her red dress, and set forth on foot for her visit to Robert de Baudricourt at Vaucouleurs. He was a rough man and at first he received her roughly. But at last she convinced him. He gave her a horse and arms and sent her to the king. She saved France."

At the rustic inn Pierre ate thick slices of dark bread and drank a stoup of thin red wine at noon. He sat at a bare table in the corner of the room. Behind him, at a table covered with a white cloth, two captains on furlough had already made their breakfast. They also were pilgrims, drawn to Domremy by the love of Jeanne d'Arc. They talked of nothing else but of her. Yet their points of view were absolutely different.

One of them, the younger, was short and swarthy, a Savoyard, the son of an Italian doctor at St. Jean de Maurienne. He was a sceptic; he believed in Jeanne, but not in the legends about her.

"I tell you," said he eagerly, "she was one of the greatest among women. But all that about her 'voices' was illusion. The priests suggested it. She had hallucinations. Remember her age when they began—just thirteen. She was clever and strong; doubtless she was pretty; certainly she was very courageous. She was only a girl. But she had a big, brave idea which possessed her—the liberation of her country. Pure? Yes. I am sure she was virtuous. Otherwise the troops would not have followed and obeyed her as they did. Soldiers are very quick about those things. They recognize and respect an honest woman. Several men were in love with her, I think. But she was *une nature froide*. The only thing that moved her was her big, brave idea—to save France. The Maid was a mother, but not of a mortal child. Her offspring was the patriotism of France."

The other captain was a man of middle age, from Lyons, the son of an architect. He was tall and pale and his large brown eyes had the tranquillity of a devout faith in them. He argued with quiet tenacity for his convictions.

"You are right to believe in her," said he, "but I think you are mistaken to deny her 'voices.' They were as real as anything in her life. You credit her when she says that she was born here, that she went to Chinon and saw the king, that delivered Orleans. Why not credit her when she says she heard God and the saints speaking to her? The proof of it was in what she did. Have you read the story of her trial? How clear and steady her answers were! The judges could not shake her. Yet at any moment she could have saved her life by denying the 'voices.' It was because she knew, because she was sure, that she could not deny. Her vision was a part of her real life. She was the mother of French patriotism—yes. But she was also the daughter of true faith. That was her power."

"Well," said the younger man, "she sacrificed herself and she saved France. That was the great thing."

"Yes," said the elder man, stretching his hand across the table to clasp the hand of his companion, "there is nothing greater than that. If we do that, God will forgive us all."

They put on their caps to go. Pierre rose and stood at attention. They returned his salute with a friendly smile and passed out.

After a few moments he finished his bread and wine, paid his score, and followed them. He watched them going down the village street toward the railway station. Then he turned and walked slowly back to the spring in the dell.

The afternoon was hot, in spite of the steady breeze which came out of the north. The air felt as if it had passed through a furnace. The low, continuous thunder of the guns rolled up from Verdun, with now and then a sharper clap from St. Mihiel.

Pierre was very tired. His head was heavy, his heart troubled. He lay down among the ferns, looking idly at the foxglove spires above him and turning over in his mind the things he had heard and seen at Domremy. Presently he fell into a profound sleep.

How long it was he could not tell, but suddenly he became aware of some one near him. He sprang up. A girl was standing beside the spring.

She wore a bright-red dress and her feet were bare. Her black hair hung down her back. Her eyes were the color of a topaz. Her form was tall and straight. She carried a distaff under her arm and looked as if she had just come from following the sheep.

"Good day, shepherdess," said Pierre. Then a strange thought struck him, and he fell on his knees. "Pardon, lady," he stammered. "Forgive my rudeness. You are of the high society of heaven, a saint. You are called Jeanne d'Arc?"

She nodded and smiled. "That is my name," said she. "Sometimes they call me *La Pucelle*, or the Maid of France. But you were right, I am a shepherdess, too. I have kept my father's sheep in the fields down there, and spun from the distaff while I watched them. I know how to sew and spin as well as any girl in the Barrois or Lorraine. Will you not stand up and talk with me?"

Pierre rose, still abashed and confused. He did not quite understand how to take this strange experience—too simple for a heavenly apparition, too real for a common dream. "Well, then," said he, "if you are a shepherdess, why are you here? There are no sheep here."

"But yes. You are one of mine. I have come here to seek you."

"Do you know me, then? How can I be one of yours?"

"Because you are a soldier of France and you are in trouble."

Pierre's head drooped. "A broken soldier," he muttered, "not fit to speak to you. I am running away because I am afraid of fear."

She threw back her head and laughed. "You speak very bad French. There is no such thing as being afraid of fear. For if you are afraid of it, you hate it. If you hate it, you will have nothing to do with it. And if you have nothing to do with it, it cannot touch you; it is nothing."

"But for you, a saint, it is easy to say that. You had no fear when you fought. You knew you would not be killed."

"I was no more sure of that than the other soldiers. Besides, when they bound me to the stake at Rouen and kindled the fire around me I knew very well that I should be killed. But there was no fear in it. Only peace."

"Ah, you were strong, a warrior born. You were not wounded and broken."

"Four times I was wounded," she answered gravely. "At Orleans a bolt went through my right shoulder. At Paris a lance tore my thigh. I never saw the blood of Frenchmen flow without feeling my heart stand still. I was not a warrior born. I knew not how to ride or fight. But I did it. What we must needs do that we can do. Soldier, do not look on the ground. Look up."

Then a strange thing took place before his eyes. A wondrous radiance, a mist of light, enveloped and hid the shepherdess. When it melted she was clad in shining armor, sitting on a white horse, and lifting a bare sword in her left hand.

"God commands you," she cried. "It is for France. Be of good cheer. Do not retreat. The fort will soon be yours!"

How should Pierre know that this was the cry with which the Maid had rallied her broken men at Orleans when the fort of *Les Tourelles* fell? What he did know was that something seemed to spring up within him to answer that call. He felt that he would rather die than desert such a leader.

The figure on the horse turned away as if to go.

"Do not leave me," he cried, stretching out his hands to her. "Stay with me. I will obey you joyfully."

She turned again and looked at him very earnestly. Her eyes shone deep into his heart. "Here I cannot stay," answered a low, sweet, womanly voice. "It is late, and my other children need me."

"But forgiveness? Can you give that to me—a coward?"

"You are no coward. Your only fault was to doubt a brave man."

"And my wife? May I go back and tell her?"

"No, surely. Would you make her hear slander of the man she loves? Be what she believes you and she will be satisfied."

"And the absolution, the word of peace? Will you speak that to me?"

Her eyes shone more clearly; the voice sounded sweeter and steadier than ever. "After the penance comes the absolution. You will find peace only at the lance's point. Son of France, go, go, go! I will help you. Go hardily to Verdun."

Pierre sprang forward after the receding figure, tried to clasp the knee, the foot of the Maid. As he fell to the ground something sharp pierced his hand. It must be her spur, thought he.

Then he was aware that his eyes were shut. He opened them and looked at his hand carefully. There was only a scratch on it, and a tiny drop of blood. He had torn it on the thorns of the wild gooseberry-bushes.

His head lay close to the clear pool of the spring. He buried his face in it and drank deep. Then he sprang up, shaking the drops from his mustache, found his cap and pistol, and hurried up the glen toward the old Roman road.

"No more of that damned foolishness about Switzerland," he said, aloud. "I belong to France. I am going with the other boys to save her. I was born for that." He took off his cap and stood still for a moment. He spoke as if he were taking an oath. "By Jeanne d'Arc!"

IV. THE VICTORIOUS PENANCE

It never occurred to Pierre Duval, as he trudged those long kilometres toward the front, that he was doing a penance.

The joy of a mind made up is a potent cordial.

The greetings of comrades on the road put gladness into his heart and strength into his legs.

It was a hot and dusty journey, and a sober one. But it was not a sad one. He was going toward that for which he was born. He was doing that which France asked of him, that which God told him to do. Josephine would be glad and proud of him. He would never be ashamed to meet her eyes. As he went, alone or in company with others, he whistled and sang a bit. He thought of *"L'Alouette"* a good deal. But not too much. He thought also of the forts of Douaumont and Vaux.

"Dame!" he cried to himself. "If I could help to win them back again! That would be fine! How sick that would make those cursed boches and their knock-kneed Crown Prince!"

At the little village of the headquarters behind Verdun he found many old friends and companions. They greeted him with cheerful irony.

"Behold the prodigal! You took your time about coming back, didn't you? Was the hospital to your taste, the nurses pretty? How is the wife? Any more children? How goes it, old man?"

"No more children yet," he answered, grinning; "but all goes well. I have come back from a far country, but I find the pigs are still grunting. What have you done to our old cook?"

"Nothing at all," was the joyous reply. "He tried to swim in his own soup and he was drowned."

When Pierre reported to the officer of the day, that busy functionary consulted the record.

"You are a day ahead of your time, Pierre Duval," he said, frowning slightly.

"Yes, sir," answered the soldier. "It costs less to be a day ahead than a day too late."

"That is well," said the officer, smiling in his red beard. "You will report to-morrow to your regiment at the citadel. You have a new colonel, but the regiment is busy in the old way."

As Pierre saluted and turned to go out his eye caught the look of a general officer who stood near, watching. He was a square, alert, vigorous man, his face bronzed by the suns of many African campaigns, his eyes full of intelligence, humor, and courage. It was Guillaumat, the new commander of the Army of Verdun.

"You are prompt, my son," said he pleasantly, "but you must remember not to be in a hurry. You have been in hospital. Are you well again? Nothing broken?"

"Something was broken, my General," responded the soldier gravely, "but it is mended."

"Good!" said the general. "Now for the front, to beat the Germans at their own game. We shall get them. It may be long, but we shall get them!"

That was the autumn of the offensive of 1916, by which the French retook, in ten days, what it had cost the Germans many months to gain.

Pierre was there in that glorious charge at the end of October which carried the heights of Douaumont and took six thousand prisoners. He was there at the recapture of the Fort de Vaux which the Germans evacuated in the first week of November. In the last rush up the slope, where he had fought long ago, a stray shell, an inscrutable messenger of fate, coming from far away, no one knows whence, caught him and ripped him horribly across the body.

It was a desperate mass of wounds. But the men of his squad loved their corporal. He still breathed. They saw to it that he was carried back to the little transit hospital just behind the Fort de Souville.

It was a rude hut of logs, covered with sand-bags, on the slope of the hill. The ruined woods around it were still falling to the crash of far-thrown shells. In the close, dim shelter of the inner room Pierre came to himself.

He looked up into the face of Father Courcy. A light of recognition and gratitude flickered in his eyes. It was like finding an old friend in the dark.

"Welcome!—But the fort?" he gasped.

"It is ours," said the priest.

Something like a smile passed over the face of Pierre. He could not speak for a long time. The blood in his throat choked him. At last he whispered:

"Tell Josephine—love."

Father Courcy bowed his head and took Pierre's hand. "Surely," he said. "But now, my dear son Pierre, I must prepare you—"

The struggling voice from the cot broke in, whispering slowly, with long intervals: "Not necessary.... I know already.... The penance. ... France.... Jeanne d'Arc.... It is done."

A few drops of blood gushed from the corner of his mouth. The look of peace that often comes to those who die of gunshot wounds settled on his face. His eyes grew still as the priest laid the sacred wafer on his lips. The broken soldier was made whole.

THE HEARING EAR

There were three American boys from the region of Philadelphia in the dugout, "Somewhere in France"; and they found it a snug habitation, considering the circumstances.

The central heating system—a round sheet-iron stove, little larger than a "topper" hat—sent out incredible quantities of acrid smoke at such times as the rusty stovepipe refused to draw. But on cold nights and frosty mornings the refractory thing was a distinct consolation. The ceiling of the apartment lacked finish. When wet it dropped mud; when dry, dust. But it had the merit of being twenty feet thick—enough to stop any German shell except a "Jack Johnson" full of high explosive. The beds were elegantly excavated in the wall, and by a slight forward inclination of the body you could use them as *fauteuils*. The rats approved of them highly.

There were two flights of ladder-stairs leading down from the trench into the dugout, and the holes at the top which served as vestibules were three or four yards apart. It was a comfort to think of this architectural design; for if the explosion of a big shell blocked up one of the entrances, the other would probably remain open, and you would not be caught in a trap with the other rats.

The main ornament of the *salon* was a neat but not gaudy biscuit-box. The top of it was a centre-table, illuminated by a single, guttering candle; the interior was a "combination" wardrobe and sideboard. Around this simple but satisfying piece of furniture the three transient tenants of the dugout had just played a game of dummy bridge, and now sat smoking and bickering as peacefully as if they were in a college club-room in America. The night on the front was what the French call *"relativement calme."* Sporadic explosions above punctuated but did not interrupt the debate, which eddied about the high theme of Education—with a capital "E"—and the particular point of dispute was the study of languages.

"Everything is going to change after the war," said Phipps-Herrick, a big Harvard man from Bryn Mawr and a member of the Unsocial Socialists' Club. "We are going to make a new world. Must have a new education. Sweep away all the old stuff—languages, grammar, literature, philosophy, history, and all that. Put in something modern and practical. Montessori system for the little kids. Vocational training for the bigger ones. Teach them to make a living. Then organize them politically and economically. You can do what you like, then, with England, France, and America together. Germany will be shut out. Why study German? From a practical point of view, I ask you, why?"

"Didn't you take it at Harvard?" sarcastically drawled Rosenlaube, a Princeton man from Rittenhouse Square. (His grandfather was born at Frankfort-on-the-Main, but his mother was a Biddle, and he had penetrated about an inch into the American diplomatic service when the war summoned him to a more serious duty.) "I understood that all you Harvard men were strong on modern languages, especially German."

Phipps-Herrick grunted.

"Certainly I took it. It was supposed to be a soft-snap course. What do you think we go to Harvard for? But that little beast, Professor von Buch, gave me a cold forty-minus on examination. So I dropped it, and thank God I've forgotten the little I ever knew of German! It will be absolutely useless in the new world."

"Right you are," said Rosenlaube. "My grandfather used to speak it when he was angry—a sloppy, slushy language, extremely ugly. At Princeton, you know, we stand by the classics, Latin and Greek, the real thing in languages. You ought to hear Dean Andy West talk about that. Of course a fellow forgets his Virgil and his Homer when he gets out in the world. But, then, he's had the benefit of them; they've given him real culture and literature. There's nothing outside of the classics, except perhaps a few things in French and Italian. Thank God I never studied German!"

The third man, who had kept silence up to this point, now gently butted in. It was little Phil Mitchell, of Overbrook, a University of Pennsylvania man, who had been stopped in his junior year by a financial catastrophe in the family, and had gone out to Idaho to earn his living as third assistant bookkeeper in a big mining concern. He took a few real books with him, besides those that he was to "keep." Double entry was his business; reading, his recreation; thinking, his vocation. From all this the great war called him as with a trumpet.

"Look here, you fellows," he said quietly, "in spite of this war and all the rest of it, there are some good things in German."

"What," they cried, "you, a fire-eater, stand up for the Kaiser and his language? Damn him!"

"With all my heart," assented Mitchell. "But the language isn't his. It existed a long while before he was born. It isn't very pretty, I'll admit. But there are lots of fine things in it. Kant and Lessing, Goethe and Schiller and Heine—they all loved liberty and made it shine out in their work. Do you mean to say that I must give them up and throw my German overboard because these modern Potsdammers have acted like brutes?"

"Yes," cried Phipps-Herrick and Rosenlaube, nodding at each other, "that's what we mean, and that's what America means. The German language must go!"

"Look here," said Phipps-Herrick, "you admit that modern education must be useful? Well, there won't be any more use for German, because we are going to shut Germany out of the international trades-union. She has betrayed the principles of the new era. We are going to boycott her."

"Won't that be rather difficult?" queried Mitchell, shaking his head. "Seventy or eighty million people—hard to shut them out of the world, eh?"

"Nonsense, dear Phil," drawled Rosenlaube; "it will be easy enough. But I don't agree with Phipps-Herrick about the reason or method. We are going to have a new era after the war. But it will not be a utilitarian age. It will be a return to beauty and form and culture—not with a 'k.' First of all, we are going to kill a great many Germans. Then we are going to Berlin to knock down all the ugly statues in the *Sieges-Allee* and smash the parvenu German Empire. Then we shall have a new age on classic lines. People will still use French and English and Italian because there is some beauty in those languages. But nobody outside of Germany will speak or read German. It is a barbarous tongue—shapeless and hideous—used by barbarians who gobble and snort when they talk. Sorry for Kant and Goethe and Heine and all that crowd, but their time is up; they've got to go out with their beastly language!"

"Yes," said Phipps-Herrick, "out with them, bag and baggage. Think what the German spies and propagandists have done in America. Schools full of pacifist and pro-German teachers; text-books full of praise of the German Empire and the Hohenzollern Highbinders; newspapers full of treason, printed in the German language. Why, it's only a piece of self-defense to clean it all out, root and branch. No more German taught or spoken, printed or read, in the United States. Forget it! Twenty-three for the Hun language!"

"Noble," gently murmured Mitchell, shaking his head again; "very noble! But not very easy and perhaps not entirely wise. Why should I throw away something that has been useful to me, and may be again? Why forget the little German that I know and burn my Goethe and refuse to listen to Beethoven's music? I won't do it, that's all."

"Our little friend is a concealed Kaiserite," said Rosenlaube. "He wants to Germanize America."

"No, Rosy," said Mitchell, thoughtfully running his hand over some nicks on the butt of his rifle in the corner; "you know I'm not a Kaiserite of any kind. I've got seven scored against him already, and I'm going to get some more. But the language question seems to me different. Cut out the German newspapers and the German schools in America by all means! No more teaching of the primary branches in any language but English! Make it absolutely necessary for everybody in the U. S. A. to learn the language of the country the first thing. Then in the high schools and universities let German be studied like any other foreign language, by those who want it—chemists, and philosophers, and historians, and electrical engineers, and so on. We could censor the text-books and keep out all complimentary allusions to the Hohenzollern family."

"Oh, shut up, Phil," growled Phipps-Herrick. "You're too soft, you old easy-mark! You don't go half far enough. We may not decide to exterminate the Hun race in Europe. But we have decided to exterminate their language in America."

His hand was groping inside the biscuit-box. He pulled out a little ditty-bag and carefully extracted a bit of newspaper.

"Listen to this, you fellows. This is from the National Obscurity Society. You know a chap with a German name is president of it, but he's a real patriot, hundred per cent, not fifty-fifty, Philly. 'The following States have abolished the teaching of German: Massachusetts, Connecticut, New York, New Jersey, Pennsylvania, Maryland, Virginia, Georgia, Mississippi, Indiana, Ohio, Illinois, Nebraska, Missouri, Kansas, Iowa, Arkansas, Arizona, Colorado, Montana, California, and Oregon.' *Abolished*, mind you! What do you think of that?"

"Most excellent Phippick," nodded Rosenlaube, "I opine, as Horace said to Cicero, 'That's the stuff,' or words to that effect. What saith the senator from Mitchellville?"

"Noble," grinned Phil, "unmistakably noble! Those Obscurity fellows are a fiery lot. It reminds me that during the late war with Spain, when I was a little, tiny boy, but brimful of ferocity, I refused to eat my favorite dessert because it was called *Spanish* cream. I felt sure at the time that my heroic conduct was of distinct assistance to Dewey in the battle of Manila Bay."

"Well, then," said Phipps-Herrick, grabbing him by the shoulders and shaking him good-humoredly, "you murderous little pacifist with seven nicks on your gun, will you give up your German? Will you forget it?"

Mitchell chuckled and shook his head,

"As far as requisite under military orders. But no further, not by a—"

A pair of muddy boots was heard and seen descending one of the ladders, followed by the manly and still rather neat form of Lieutenant Barker Bunn, a Cornell man from West Philadelphia. The three men sprang to their feet and saluted smartly, for the lieutenant was very stiff about all the preliminary forms.

"Too loud talking here," he said gruffly. "I heard you before I came down. Who is here? Oh, I see, Sergeant Phipps-Herrick, Privates Rosenlaube and Mitchell. It's your turn to go out on listening post to-night, sergeant. Twelve sharp, stay three hours, go as far as you can, come back and report, take Mitchell or Rosenlaube with you. Captain's orders."

The sergeant saluted again, and the two men looked at each other.

"Why not both of us, sir?" said Mitchell.

The lieutenant regarded him with some surprise. Listening post is not a detail passionately desired by the men. It is always dirty, frequently dangerous, generally obscure, and often fatal. Hence there is no keen competition for it.

"Two is the usual number for a listening post," said Barker Bunn thoughtfully. "But there is no regulation about it, and the captain did not specify any number. Well, yes, I suppose you can all three go, if you are set on it. In fact, I give the order to that effect."

"Thank you, sir," said Rosenlaube and Mitchell. Phipps-Herrick, feeling that the strict etiquette of the preliminaries had been fully observed and the time to be human had come, held out a box of "Fierce Fairies."

"Have a cigarette, Bunn, and take a chair, do. Time for a little talk this quiet night? Tell us what's doing up above."

"Nothing particular," said Barker Bunn, lighting and relaxing. "But the old man has a hunch that the Fritzies are grubbing a mine—a corker—to get our goat. Hence this business of ears forward. The old man thinks the Fritzies have a strong grouch against this little alley, and since they couldn't take it top side last week they're going to try to bust it out bottom side with a big bang some day soon. Maybe so—maybe just greens—but, anyway, you've got to go on the Q. T. with this job—no noise, don't even whisper unless you have to; just listen for all you're worth. P'r'aps you'll hear that little tap-tap-tapping that tells where Fritzie Mole is at work. Then if you come back and tell the old man where it is, he'll give you all the cigarettes you want. But say, do you want me to give you a pointer on the way to go, the method of procedure, as the old man would call it?"

They agreed that they were thirsting for information and instruction.

"Well, it's this way," continued Barker Bunn. "You know I had a bit of experience in listening post while I was with the Canadians down around 'Wipers'; and I noticed that most of the troubles came from a bad method of procedure. Fellows went out any old way; followed each other in the dark, and then hunted for each other and came to grief; all those kind of silly fumbles. Now, what you need is *formation*—see? Must have some sort of formation for advance. Must keep in touch. For two men a tandem is right. For three men, what you want is a spike-team—middle man crawls ahead, other men follow on each side just near enough to touch his left heel with right hand and right heel with left hand—a triangle, see? Keep touching once every thirty seconds. If you miss it, leader crawls back, side men crawl in, sure to meet, nobody gets lost. Go as far *as* you can, then spread out like a fan, fold together *when* you can, come back *if* you can—that's the way to cover the most possible ground on a listening post. Do you get me?"

"We get you," they nodded. "It's a wonderful scheme." And Rosenlaube added in his most impressive literary manner: "Plato, it *must* be so, thou reasonest well."

"But tell me," said the lieutenant, "what were you fellows chattering about so loud when I came down?"

So they told him, and, according to the habit of college boys, they skirmished over the ground of debate again, and Barker Bunn vigorously supported the majority opinion, and Mitchell was left in a hopeless minority of one, clinging obstinately to his faith that there had been, and still might be, some use for the German language.

Midnight came, and with it the return of the lieutenant's official manner. He saw the trio slide over the top, one by one, vanishing in the starless dark. "Good luck going and coming," he whispered; and it sounded almost like an unofficial prayer.

In single file they crept through the prepared opening in the barbed-wire entanglement, and so out into No Man's Land, where they took up their spike-team formation. Phipps-Herrick was the leader, the other men were the wheelers. They had agreed on a code of silent signals: One kick with the heel or one pinch with the hand meant "stop"; two meant "back"; three meant "get together." They carried no rifles, because the rifle is an awkward tool for a noiseless crawler to lug. But each man had a big trench-knife and a pair of automatic pistols, with plenty of ammunition.

The space between the two front lines of barbed wire in this region was not more than four or five hundred yards. In the murk of that unstarred, drizzling night, where every inch must be felt out, it seemed like a vast, horrible territory. There was nothing monotonous about it but the blackness of darkness. To the touch it was a *paysage accidente*, a landscape full of surprises. Dead bodies were sprinkled over it. It was pockmarked with small shell-holes and pitted with large craters, many of them full of water, all slimy with mud. Phipps-Herrick nearly slipped into one of the deepest, but a lively kick warned his followers of the danger, and they pulled him back by the heels.

Now and then a star-shell looped across the spongy sky, casting a lurid illumination over the ghastly field. When the three travellers caught the soft swish of its ascent, they "froze"—motionless as a shamming 'possum—mimicking death among the dead.

It was a long, slow, silent, revolting crawl. Sounds which did not concern them were plenty—distant cannonade, shells exploding here and there, scattered rifle-shots. All these they unconsciously eliminated, listening for something else, ears pressed to the ground wherever they could find a comparatively dry spot. From their point of hearing the night was still as the grave—no subterranean tapping and scraping could they hear anywhere under the sea of mud.

Once Rosenlaube caught a faint metallic sound, and signalled through Phipps-Herrick's left leg to Mitchell's left arm, "Stop!" All three listened tensely. They crawled toward the faint noise. It was made by a loose end of wire swaying in the night-wind and tapping on a broken helmet.

They were getting close to the German barbed wire. The leader had swung around to the west, following what he judged to be the line of the front trench, perhaps forty yards away. He was determined to hear something before he went back. And he did!

Just as he had made up his mind to call up the other fellows for the final spreadout in fan formation, his groping right hand touched something round and smooth and hard. It seemed to be made fast to a string or wire, but he pulled it toward him and gave the "stop" signal to his followers.

The thing he had picked up was a telephone receiver. How it came to be there he did not know. Perhaps a German listening post had carried it out last night, in order to receive directions from the trench; perhaps the mining party—man killed, receiver dropped, wire connection not cut, or tangled up with other wires—who can tell? One thing is sure—here is the receiver, faintly buzzing. Phipps-Herrick joyfully puts it to his ear. He hears a voice and words, but it is all gibberish to him. With a look of desperation on his face he gives the "get together" signal.

Rosenlaube crawls up first and takes hold of the cylinder, puts it to his ear. He hears the sound, but it says absolutely nothing to him. It is like being at the door of the secret of the universe and unable to get over the threshold.

Then comes Mitchell, slowly, a little lame, and almost "all in." Phipps-Herrick thrusts the receiver into his hand. As he listens a beatific expression spreads over his face. It lasts a long time, and then he lays down the cylinder with a sigh.

The three heads are close together, and Mitchell whispers under his breath:

"Got 'em—got the whole thing—line of mine changed—raiders coming out now—twelve men—rough on us, but if we can get back to our alley we've got 'em! Crawl home quick."

{Illustration with caption: "I'm going to carry you in, spite of hell"}

They crawled together in a bunch, formation ignored. Presently steps sounded near them. A swift light swept the hole where they crouched, a volley of rifle-shots crashed into it. The Americans answered with their pistols, and saw three or four of the dark forms on the edge of the hole topple over. The rest disappeared. But Rosenlaube had a rifle-ball through his right hip and another through his shoulder. Mitchell and Phipps-Herrick started to carry him.

"Drop it," he whispered. "I'm safe here till dawn—you get home, quick! Specially Phil. He's the one that counts. Cut away, boys!"

Meantime the American trench had opened fire and the German trench answered. The still night broke into a tempest of noise. A bullet or a bit of shell caught Mitchell in the knee and crumpled him up. Phipps-Herrick lifted him on his back and stood up.

"Come on," he said, "you little cuss. You're the only one that has the stuff we went out after. I'm going to carry you in, 'spite of hell."

And he did it.

Mitchell told the full story of the change in the direction of the German mine and the plan of the next assault, as he had heard it through that lost receiver. The captain said it was information of the highest value. It counted up to a couple of hundred German prisoners and three machine-guns in the next two days.

Rosenlaube, still alive, was brought in just before daybreak by a volunteer rescue-party under the guidance of Phipps-Herrick. All three were cited in the despatches. Phipps-Herrick in due time received the Distinguished Service Cross for gallantry on the field. But Mitchell had the surplus satisfaction of the hearing ear.

"Look here, old man," Rosenlaube said to him as they lay side by side in the hospital, "member our talk in the dugout just before our big night? Well, I allow there was something in what you said. There are times when it is a good thing to know a bit of that barbarous German language. And you never can tell when one of those times may hit you."

SKETCHES OF QUEBEC

If you love a certain country, for its natural beauty, or for the friends you have made there, or for the happy days you have passed within its borders, you are troubled and distressed when that country comes under criticism, suspicion, and reproach.

It is just as it would be if a woman who had been very kind to you and had done you a great deal of good were accused of some unworthiness. You would refuse to believe it. You would insist on understanding before you pronounced judgment. Memories would ask to be heard.

That is what I feel in regard to French Canada, the province of Quebec, where I have had so many joyful times, and found so many true comrades among the *voyageurs*, the *habitants*, and the *coureurs de bois*.

People are saying now that Quebec is not loyal, not brave, not patriotic in this war for freedom and humanity.

Even if the accusation were true, of course it would not spoil the big woods, the rushing rivers, the sparkling lakes, the friendly mountains of French Canada. But all the same, it hurts me to hear such a charge against my friends of the forest.

Do you mean to tell me that Francois and Ferdinand and Louis and Jean and Eugene and Iside are not true men? Do you mean to tell me that these lumbermen who steer big logs down steep places, these trappers who brave the death-cold grip of Winter, these canoe-men who shout for joy as they run the foaming rapids,—do you mean to tell me that they have no courage?

I am not ready to credit that. I want to hear what they have to say for themselves. And in listening for that testimony certain little remembrances come to me—not an argument—only a few sketches on the wall. Here they are. Take them for what they are worth.

I

LA GRANDE DECHARGE

September, 1894

In one of the long stillwaters of the mighty stream that rushes from *Lac Saint Jean* to make the Saguenay—below the *Ile Maligne* and above the cataract of Chicoutimi—two birch-bark canoes are floating quietly, descending with rhythmic strokes of the paddle, through the luminous northern twilight.

The chief guide, Jean Morel, is a *coureur de bois* of the old type—broad-shouldered, red-bearded, a fearless canoeman, a good hunter and fisherman—simple of speech and deep of heart: a good man to trust in the rapids.

"Tell me, Jean," I ask in the comfortable leisure of our voyage which conduces to pipe-smoking and conversation, "tell me, are you a Frenchman or an Englishman?"

"Not the one, nor the other," answers Jean in his old-fashioned *patois*. "M'sieu' knows I am French-Canadian."

A remarkable answer, when you come to think of it; for it claims a nationality which has never existed, and is not likely to exist, except in a dream.

"Well, then," I say, following my impulse of psychological curiosity, of which Jean is sublimely ignorant, "suppose a war should come between France and England. On which side would you fight?"

Jean knocks the dottle out of his pipe, refills and relights. Then, between the even strokes of his paddle, he makes this extraordinary reply:

"M'sieu, I suppose my body would march under the flag of England. But my heart would march under the flag of France."

Good old Jean Morel! You had no premonition of this glorious war in which the Tricolor and the Union Jack would advance together against the ravening black eagle of Germany, and the Stars and Stripes would join them.

How should you know anything about it? Your log cabin was your capitol. Your little family was your council of state. Even the rest of us, proud of our university culture, were too blind, in those late Victorian days, to see the looming menace of Prussian paganism and the conquer-lust of the Hohenzollerns, which has plunged the whole world in war.

II

OXFORD

February, 1917

The "Schools" building, though modern, is one of the stateliest on the Main Street. Here, in old peaceful times, the university examinations used to be held. Now it is transformed into a hospital for the wounded men from the fighting front of freedom.

Sir William Osier, Canadian, and world-renowned physician, is my guide, an old friend in Baltimore, now Regius Professor of Medicine in Oxford.

"Come," he says, "I want you to see an example of the Carrel treatment of wounds."

The patient is sitting up in bed—a fine young fellow about twenty years old. A shrapnel-shell, somewhere in France, passed over his head and burst just behind him. His bare back is a mass of scars. The healing fluid is being pumped in through the shattered elbow of his right arm, not yet out of danger.

"Does it hurt," I ask.

"Not much," he answers, trying to smile, "at least not too much, M'sieu'."

The accent of French Canada is unmistakable. I talk to him in his own dialect.

"What part of Quebec do you come from?"

"From *Trois Rivieres*, M'sieu', or rather from a country back of that, the Saint Maurice River."

"I know it well—often hunted there. But what made you go to the war?"

"I heard that England fought to save France from the damned Germans. That was enough, M'sieu', to make me march. Besides, I always liked to fight."

"What did you do before you became a soldier?"

"I was a lumberjack."

(What he really said was, *"J'allais en chantier,"* "I went in the shanty." If he had spoken in classic French he would have said, *"J'etais bucheron."* How it brought back the smell of the big spruce forest to hear that word *chantier*, in Oxford!)

{Illustration: "I was a lumberjack."}

"Well, then, I suppose you will return to the wood-cutting again, when this war is over."

"But no, M'sieu', how can I, with this good-for-nothing arm? I shall never be capable of swinging the axe again."

"But you could be the cook, perfectly. And you know the cook gets the best pay in the whole shanty."

His face lights up a little.

"Truly," he replies; "I never thought of that, but it is true. I have seen a bit of cooking at the front and learned some things. I might take up that end of the job. *But anyway, Im glad I went to the war."*

So we say good-by—*"bonne chance!"*

Since that day the good physician who guided me through the hospital has borne without a murmur the greatest of all sacrifices—the loss of his only son, a brave and lovely boy, killed in action against the thievish, brutal German hordes.

III

SAINTE MARGUERITE August, 1917

The wild little river *Sainte Marguerite* runs joyously among the mountains and the green woods, back of the Saguenay, singing the same old song of liberty and obedience to law, as if the world had never been vexed and tortured by the madness of war-lords.

A tired man who has a brief furlough from active service is lucky if he can spend it among the big trees and beside a flowing stream. The trees are ministers of peace. The stream is full of courage and adventure as it rushes toward the big sea.

We are coming back to camp from the morning's fishing, with a brace of good salmon in the canoe.

"Tell me, Iside," I ask of the wiry little bowman, the best hunter and fisher on the river, "why is it that you are not at the war?"

"But, M'sieu', I am too old. A father of family—almost a grandfather—the war is not for men of that age. Besides, it does not concern us here in Quebec."

"Why not? It concerns the whole world. Who told you that it does not concern you?"

"The priest at our village of *Sacre Coeur*, M'sieu'. He says that it is only right and needful for a good Christian to fight in defense of his home and his church. Let those Germans attack us here, *chez nous*, and you shall see how the men of *Sacre Coeur* will stand up and fight."

It was an amazing revelation of a state of mind, absolutely simple, perfectly sincere, and strictly imprisoned by the limitations of its only recognized teacher.

"But suppose, Iside, that England and France should be beaten down by Germany, over there. What would happen to French Canada? Do you think you could stand alone then, to defend your home and your church? Are you big enough, you French-Canadians?"

"M'sieu', I have never thought of that. Perhaps we have more than a million people—many of them children, for you understand we French-Canadians have large families—but of course the children could not fight. Still, we should not like to have them subject to a German Emperor. We would fight against that, if the war came to us here on our own soil."

"But don't you see that the only way to keep it from coming to you on your own soil is to fight against it over there? Hasn't the English Government given you all your liberties, for home and church?"

"Yes, M'sieu', especially since Sir Wilfred Laurier. Ah, that is a great man! A true French-Canadian!"

"Well, then, you know that he is against Germany. You know he believes the freedom of Canada depends on the defeat of Germany, over there, on the other side of the sea. You would not like a German Canada, would you?"

"Not at all, M'sieu', that would be intolerable. But I have never thought of that."

"Well, think of it now, will you? And tell your priest to think of it, too. He is a Christian. The things we are fighting for belong to Christianity—justice, liberty, humanity. Tell him that, and tell him also some of the things which the Germans did to the Christian people in Belgium and Northern France. I will narrate them to you later."

"M'sieu'," says Iside, dipping his paddle deeper as we round the sharp corner of a rock, "I shall remember all that you tell me, and I shall tell it again to our priest. You know we have few newspapers here. Most of us could not read them, anyway. I am not well convinced that we yet comprehend, here in French Canada, the meaning of this war. But we shall endeavor to comprehend it better. And when we comprehend, we shall be ready to do our duty—you can trust yourself to the men of *Sacre Coeur* for that. We love peace—we all about here *(nous autres d'icite)—but we can fight like the devil when we know it is for a good cause—liberty, for example.* Meanwhile would M'sieu' like to stop at the pool *'La Pinette"* on the way down and try a couple of casts? There was a big salmon rising there yesterday."

That very evening a runner comes up the river, through the woods, to tell Iside and Eugene, who are Selectmen of the community of *Sacre Coeur*, that they must come down to the village for an important meeting at ten o'clock the next morning.

So they set off, quite as a matter of course, for their thirty-five mile tramp through the forest in the dark. They are good citizens, as well as good woodsmen, you understand. On the second day they are back again at their work in the canoe.

"Well, Iside," I ask, "how was it with the meeting yesterday? All correct?"

"All correct, M'sieu'. It was an affair of a new schoolhouse. We are going to build it. All goes well. We are beginning to comprehend. Quebec is a large corner of the world. But it is only a corner, after all, we can see that. And those damned Germans who do such terrible things in France, we do not love them at all, no matter what the priest may say about Christian charity. They are Protestants, M'sieu', is it not?"

"Well," I answer, hiding a smile with a large puff of smoke, "some of them call themselves Protestants and some call themselves Catholics. But it seems to me they are all infidels, heathen—judging by what they do. That is the real proof."

"*C'est b'en vrai, M'sieu'*," says Iside. "It is the conduct that shows the Christian."

IV

BELOW CAPE DIAMOND March, 1818

The famous citadel of Quebec stands on top of the steep hill that dominates the junction of the Saint Charles River with the Saint Lawrence. That is Cape Diamond—a natural stronghold. Indians and French, and British, and Americans have fought for that coign of vantage. For a century and a half the Union Jack has floated there, and under its fair protection the Province of Quebec, keeping its quaint old language and peasant customs, has become an important part of the British Empire.

The Upper Town, on the high shoulders of Cape Diamond, with its government buildings, convents, hospitals, showy new shops, and ancient gardens, its archiepiscopal palace, trim theological seminary, huge castle-like hotel, and placid ramparts dominating the *Ile d'Orleans* with rows of antiquated, harmless cannon around which the children play—the Upper Town belongs distinctly to the citadel. The garrison is in evidence here. A regimental band plays in the kiosk on Dufferin Terrace on summer evenings. There is a good mixture of khaki in the coloring of the street crowd, and many wounded soldiers are seen, invalided home from the front. They are all very proud of the glorious record that Canada has made in the battle for freedom. Most of them, it seems to me, are from English-speaking families. But by no means all. There are many of unmistakable French-Canadian stock; and they tell me proudly of the notable bravery of a certain regiment which was formed early from volunteers of their own people—hunters, woodsmen, farmers, guides. The war does not seem very far away, up here in the region of the citadel.

The Lower Town, with its narrow streets, little shops, gray stone warehouses, dingy tenements, and old-fashioned markets, is quite a different place. It belongs to the slow rivers on whose banks it drowses and dreams. The once prosperous lumberyards are half empty now. The shipping along the wharfs has been dwindling for many years. The northern winter puts a quietus on the waterside. Troops, munitions, supplies, must go down by rail to an ice-free port. The white river-boats are all laid up. But a way is kept open across the river to Levis, and the sturdy, snub-nosed little ice-breaking ferry-boats buffet back and forth almost without interruption. There is a plenty of nothing to do, now, in the Lower Town; pipe-smoking and heated discussion of parish politics are incessant; an inconsiderate quantity of bad liquor is imbibed, *pour faire passer le temps*.

Suddenly—if anything can be said to happen suddenly in Quebec—bad news comes from the Lower Town. A riot has broken out, an insurrection of the French-Canadians against the new military service act, an armed resistance to the draft. Windows have been smashed, shops looted. A mob, not very large perhaps, but extremely noisy, has marched up the steep curve of Mountain Hill Street, into the Upper Town. Shots have been exchanged. People have been killed. The revolution in Quebec has begun.

That is the disquieting rumor which comes to us, carefully spread and magnified by those agencies which have an interest in preventing, or at least obstructing the righteous punishment of the German criminals in this war. Can it possibly be true? Have the French-Canadians gone crazy, as the Irish did in 1916, under the lunatic incantations of the Sinn-Feiners? Are they also people without a country, playing blindly into the hands of the Prussian gang who have set out to subjugate the world?

No! This riot in the old city is not an expression of the spirit of French Canada at all. It is only a shrewdly stupid trick in local politics, planned and staged by small-minded and loud-voiced politicians who are trying to keep their hold upon the province. The so-called revolutionists are either imported loafers and trouble-makers, or else they are drawn from that class of "hooligans" who have always made a noise around the Quebec hotels at night. They shout much: they swear abominably: but they have no real fight in them. They can be hired and used—up to a certain point—but beyond that they are worthless. It is a waste of money to employ them. The trouble below Cape Diamond froths up and goes down as quickly as the effervescence on a bottle of ginger beer. Before you can find out what it is all about, it is all over. It has not even touched the real French-Canadians, the men of the forests and the farms. They are loyal by nature, and slow by temperament. You have got to give them time, and light.

What is happening in Quebec now? Just what ought to happen. The draft is going forward smoothly and steadily, without resistance. Sons of the best French-Canadian families are volunteering for the war. Recruits from Laval University are coming in, stirred perhaps by the knowledge that forty thousand Catholic priests in France have entered the army which fights against the Prussian paganism.

The petty politicians who have sought to serve their own ends by putting forward the mad notion of secession and an independent "Republic of Quebec" have gone to cover under a storm of ridicule and indignation. M. Bourassa's iridescent dream of French-Canadian nationalism has disappeared like a soap-bubble. M. Francoeur's motion in the Quebec legislature, carrying a vague hint that the province might withdraw from the Dominion if the other provinces were not particularly nice to it, was snowed under by an overwhelming vote. The patriotic and eloquent speech of the provincial Premier, M. Gouin, was received with every sign of approval. The political cinema has shown its latest film, and the title is evidently *"Fidelite de Quebec."*

Meantime a Catholic missioner has been in the province. The visit of Archbishop Mathieu of Saskatchewan was probably made on the invitation, certainly with the consent, of the hierarchy of Quebec. That intelligent and fearless preacher brought with him a clear and ringing gospel, a call to all Christian folk to stand up together and "resist even unto blood, striving against sin"—the sin of the German war-lords who have plunged the world in agony to enforce their heresy that Might makes Right.

Such a message, at this time, must be of inestimable value to the humble and devout people of the province, attached as they are to their church, and looking patiently to her for guidance. The parish priests, devoted to their lonely tasks in obscure hamlets, may get a new and broader inspiration from it. They may have a vision of the ashes of Louvain University, the ruin of Rheims Cathedral, wrought by ruthless German hands. Then the church in Quebec will measure up to the church in Belgium and in France. Then the village cure will say to his young men: "Go! Fight! It is for the glory of God and the good of the world. It is for the Christian religion and the life of free Canada."

"Well, then," says the gentle reader, of a sociological turn of mind, who has followed me thus far, "what have you got to say about the big political problem of Quebec? Is a French-speaking province a safe factor in the Dominion of Canada, in the British Empire? Why was Quebec so late in coming into this world war against Germany?"

Dear man, I have nothing whatever to say about what you call the big political problem of Quebec. I told you that at the beginning. That is a question for Canada and Great Britain to settle. The British colonial policy has always been one of the greatest liberality and fairness, except perhaps in that last quarter of the eighteenth century, when the madness of a German king and his ministers in England forced the United States to break away from her, and form the republic which has now become her most powerful friend.

The perpetuation of a double language within a state, an *enclave*, undoubtedly carries with it an element of inconvenience and possibly of danger. Yet Belgium is bilingual and Switzerland is quadrilingual. If any tongue other than that of the central government is to be admitted, what could be better than French—the language of culture, which has spoken the large words, *liberte, egalite, fraternite?* The native dialect of French Canada is a quaint and delightful thing—an eighteenth-century vocabulary with pepper and salt from the speech of the woodsmen and hunters. I should be sorry if it had to fade out. But evidently that is a question for Canada to decide. She has been a bilingual country for a long time. I see no reason why the experiment should not be carried on.

Quebec has been rather slow in waking up to the meaning of this war for world-freedom. But she has been very little slower than some of the United States, after all.

The Church? Well, the influence of the Church always has depended and always must depend upon the quality of her ministers. In France, in Belgium, they have not fallen short of their high duty. The Archbishop of Saskatchewan, who came to Quebec, preached a clear gospel of self-sacrifice for a righteous cause.

But the plain people of Quebec—the *voyageurs*, the *habitants*, my old friends in the back districts—that is what I am thinking about. I am sure they are all right. They are very simple, old-fashioned, childish, if you like; but there is no pacifist or pro-German virus among them. If their parochial politicians will let them alone, if their priests will speak to them as prophets of the God of Righteousness, they will show their mettle. They will prove their right to be counted among the free peoples of the world who are willing to defend peace with arms.

That is what I expect to find if I ever get back to my canoemen on the *Sainte Marguerite* again.

SYLVANORA, July 10, 1918.

A CLASSIC INSTANCE

"Latin and Greek are dead," said Hardman, lean, eager, absolute, a fanatic of modernity. "They have been a long while dying, and this war has finished them. We see now that they are useless in the modern world. Nobody is going to waste time in studying them. Education must be direct and scientific. Train men for efficiency and prepare them for defense. Otherwise they will have no chance of making a living or of keeping what they make. Your classics are musty and rusty and fusty. *Heraus mit*——"

He checked himself suddenly, with as near a blush as his sallow skin could show.

"Excuse me," he stammered; "bad habit, contracted when I was a student at Kiel—only place where they really understood metallurgy."

Professor John De Vries, round, rosy, white-haired, steeped in the mellow lore of ancient history, puffed his cigar and smiled that benignant smile with which he was accustomed joyfully to enter a duel of wits. Many such conflicts had enlivened that low-ceilinged book-room of his at Calvinton.

"You are excused, my dear Hardman," he said, "especially because you have just given us a valuable illustration of the truth that language and the study of language have a profound influence upon thought. The tongue which you inadvertently used belongs to the country that bred the theory of education which you advocate. The theory is as crude and imperfect as the German language itself. And that is saying a great deal."

Young Richard De Vries, the professor's favorite nephew and adopted son, whose chief interest was athletics, but who had a very pretty side taste for verbal bouts, was sitting with the older men before a cheerful fire of logs in the chilly spring of 1917. He tucked one leg comfortably underneath him and leaned forward in his chair, lighting a fresh cigarette. He foresaw a brisk encounter, and was delighted, as one who watches from the side-lines the opening of a lively game.

"Well played, sir," he ejaculated; "well played, indeed. Score one for you, Uncle."

"The approbation of the young is the consolation of the aged," murmured the professor sententiously, as if it were a quotation from Plutarch. "But let us hear what our friend Hardman has to say about the German language and the Germanic theory of education. It is his turn."

"I throw you in the German language," answered Hardman, rather tartly. "I don't profess to admire it or defend it. But nobody can deny its utility for the things that are taught in it. You can learn more science from half a dozen recent German books than from a whole library of Latin and Greek. Besides, you must admit that the Germans are great classical scholars too."

"Rather neat," commented Dick; "you touched him there, Mr. Hardman. Now, Uncle!"

"I do not admit," said the professor firmly, "that the Germans are great classical scholars. They are great students, that is all. The difference is immense. Far be it from me to deny the value of the patient and laborious researches of the Germans in the grammar and syntax of the ancient languages and in archaeology. They are painstaking to a painful degree. They gather facts as bees gather pollen, indefatigably. But when it comes to making honey they go dry. They cannot interpret, they can only instruct. They do not comprehend, they only classify. Name me one recent German book of classical interpretation to compare in sweetness and light with Jowett's 'Dialogues of Plato' or Butcher's 'Some Aspects of the Greek Genius' or Croiset's 'Histoire de la Litterature Grecque.' You can't do it," he ended, with a note of triumph.

"Of course not," replied Hardman sharply. "I never claimed to know anything about classical literature or scholarship. My point at the beginning—you have cleverly led the discussion away from it, like one of your old sophists—the point I made was that Greek and Latin are dead languages, and therefore practically worthless in the modern world. Let us go back to that and discuss it fairly and leave the Germans out."

"But that, my dear fellow, is precisely what you cannot do. It is partly because they have insisted on treating Latin and Greek as dead that the Germans have become what they are—spectacled barbarians, learned Huns, veneered Vandals. In older times it was not so bad. They had some perception of the everlasting current of life in the classics. When the Latin spirit touched them for a while, they acquired a sense of form, they produced some literature that was good—Lessing, Herder, Goethe, Schiller. But it was a brief illumination, and the darkness that followed it was deeper than ever. Who are their foremost writers to-day? The Hauptmanns and the Sudermanns, gropers in obscurity, violent sentimentalists, 'bigots to laxness,' Dr. Johnson would have called them. Their world is a moral and artistic chaos agitated by spasms of hysteria. Their work is a mass of decay touched with gleams of phosphorescence. The Romans would have called it *immunditia*. What is your new American word for that kind of thing, Richard? I heard you use it the other day."

"Punk," responded Dick promptly. "Sometimes, if it's very sickening, we call it pink punk."

"All right," interrupted Hardman impatiently. "Say what you like about Hauptmann and Sudermann. They are no friends of mine. Be as ferocious with them as you please. But you surely do not mean to claim that the right kind of study and understanding of the classics could have had any practical influence on the German character, or any value in saving the German Empire from its horrible blunders."

"Precisely that is what I do mean."

"But how?"

"Through the mind, *animus*, the intelligent directing spirit which guides human conduct in all who have passed beyond the stage of mere barbarism."

"You exaggerate the part played by what you call the mind. Human conduct is mainly a matter of heredity and environment. Most of it is determined by instinct, impulse, and habit."

"Granted, for the sake of argument. But may there not be a mental as well as a physical inheritance, an environment of thought as well as of bodily circumstances?"

"Perhaps so. Yes, I suppose that is true to a certain extent."

"A poor phrase, my dear Hardman; but let it pass. Will you admit that there may be habits of thinking and feeling as well as habits of doing and making things?"

"Certainly."

"And do you recognize a difference between bad habits and good habits?"

"Of course."

"And you agree that this difference exists both in mental and in physical affairs? For example, you would call the foreman of a machine-shop who directed his work in accordance with the natural laws of his material and of his steam or electric power a man of good habits, would you not?"

"Undoubtedly."

"And you would not deny him this name, but would rather emphasize it, if in addition he had the habit of paying regard to the moral and social laws which condition the welfare and efficiency of his workmen; for example, self-control, cheerfulness, honesty, fair play, honor, human kindness, and so on. If he taught these things, not only by word but by deed, you would call him an excellent foreman, would you not?"

"Without a question. That machine-shop would be a great success, a model."

"But suppose your foreman had none of these good mental and moral habits. Suppose he was proud, overbearing, dishonest, unfair, and cruel. Do you not believe he would have a bad influence upon his men? Would not the shop, no matter what kind of work it turned out, become a nest of evil and a menace to its neighbors?"

"It surely would."

"What, then, would you do with the foreman?"

"I would try to teach him better. If that failed, I would discharge him."

"In what method and by what means would you endeavor to teach him?"

"By all the means that I could command. By precept and by example, by warning him of his faults and by showing him better ways, by wholesome books and good company."

"And if he refused to learn; if he remained obstinate; if he mocked you and called you a hypocrite; if he claimed that his way was the best, in fact the only way, divinely inspired, and therefore beyond all criticism, then you would throw him out?"

"Certainly, and quickly! I should regard him as morally insane, and try my best to put him where he could do no more harm. But tell me why this protracted imitation of Socrates? Where are you trying to lead me? Do you want me to say that the German Kaiser is a very bad foreman of his shop; that he has got it into a horrible mess and made it despised and hated by all the other shops; that he ought to be put out? If that is your point, I am with you in advance."

"Right you are!" cried Dick joyously. "Can the Kaiser! We all agree to that. And here the bout ends, with honors for both sides, and a special prize for the Governor."

The professor smiled, recognizing in the name more affection than disrespect. He leaned forward in his chair, lighting a fresh cigar with gusto.

"Not yet," he said, "O too enthusiastic youth! Our friend here has not yet come to the point at which I was aiming. The application of my remarks to the Kaiser—whom I regard as a gifted paranoiac—is altogether too personal and limited. I was thinking of something larger and more important. Do you give me leave to develop the idea?"

"Fire away, sir," said Dick.

Hardman nodded his assent. "I should like very much to hear in what possible way you connect the misconduct of Germany, which I admit, with your idea of the present value of classical study, which I question."

"In this way," said the professor earnestly. "Germany has been living for fifty years with a closed mind. Oh, I grant you it was an active mind, scientific, laborious, immensely patient. But it was an ingrowing mind. Sure of its own superiority, it took no counsel with antiquity and scorned the advice of its neighbors. It was intent on producing something entirely new and all its own—a purely German *Kultur*, independent of the past, and irresponsible to any laws except those of Germany's interests and needs. Hence it fell into bad habits of thought and feeling, got into trouble, and brought infinite trouble upon the world."

"And do you claim," interrupted Hardman, "that this would have been prevented by reading the classics? Would that have been the only and efficient cure for Germany's disease? Rather a large claim, that!"

"Much too large," replied the professor. "I did not make it. In the first place, it may be that Germany's trouble had gone beyond any cure but the knife. In the second place, I regard the intelligent reading of the Bible and the vital apprehension of the real spirit of Christianity as the best of all cures for mental and moral ills. All that I claim for the classics—the works of the greatest of the Greek and Roman writers—is that they have in them a certain remedial and sanitary quality. They contain noble thoughts in noble forms. They show the strength of self-restraint. They breathe the air of clearness and candor. They set forth ideals of character and conduct which are elevating. They also disclose the weakness and the ugliness of things mean and base. They have the broad and generous spirit of the true *literae humaniores*. They reveal the springs of civilization and lead us—

'To the glory that was Greece,

To the grandeur that was Rome.'

Now these are precisely the remedies 'indicated,' as the physicians say, for the cure, or at least the mitigation, of the specific bad habits which finally caused the madness of Germany."

"Please tell us, sir," asked Dick gravely, "how you mean us to take that. Do you really think it would have done any good to those brutes who ravaged Belgium and outraged France to read Tacitus or Virgil or the Greek tragedies? They couldn't have done it, anyhow."

"Probably not," answered the professor, while Hardman sat staring intently into the fire, "probably not. But suppose the leaders and guides of Germany (her masters, in effect, who moulded and *kultured* the people to serve their nefarious purpose of dominating the world by violence), suppose these masters had really known the meaning and felt the truth of the Greek tragedies, which unveil reckless arrogance—*Hybris*—as the fatal sin, hateful to the gods and doomed to an inevitable Nemesis. Might not this truth, filtering through the masters to the people, have led them to the abatement of the ruinous pride which sent Germany out to subjugate the other nations in 1914? The egregious General von der Goltz voiced the insane arrogance which made this war when he said, 'The nineteenth century saw a German Empire, the twentieth shall see a German world.'

"Or suppose the Teutonic teachers and pastors had read with understanding and taken to heart the passages of Csesar in which he curtly describes the violent and thievish qualities of the ancient Germans—how they spread desolation around them to protect their borders, and encouraged their young men in brigandage in order to keep them in practice. Might not these plain lessons have been used as a warning to the people of modern Germany to discourage their predatory propensities and their habits of devastation and to hold them back from their relapse into the *Schrecklichkeit* of savage warfare? George Meredith says a good thing in 'Diana of the Crossways': 'Before you can civilize a man, you must first de-barbarize him.' That is the trouble with the Germans, especially their leaders and masters. They have never gotten rid of their fundamental barbarism, the idolatry of might above right.

They have only put on a varnish of civilization.

It cracks and peels off in the heat.

"Take one more illustration. Suppose these German thought-masters and war-lords had really understood and assimilated the true greatness of the conception of the old Roman Empire as it is shown, let us say, by Virgil. You remember that splendid passage in the Sixth Book of the AEneid where the Romans are called to remember that it is their mission 'to crown Peace with Law, to spare the humbled, and to subdue and tame the proud.' Might not sucn a noble doctrine have detached the Germans a little from their blind devotion to the Hohenzollern-Hollweg conception of the modern pinchbeck German Empire—a predatory state, greedy to gain new territory but incapable of ruling it when gained, scornful of the rights of smaller peoples, oppressing them when subjugated, as she has oppressed Poland and Schleswig-Holstein and Alsace-Lorraine, a clumsy and exterminating tyrant in her own colonies, as she has shown herself in East and West Africa? I tell you that a vital perception of what the Roman Empire really meant in its palmy days might have been good medicine for Germany. It might have taught her to make herself fit for power before seeking to grasp it."

"Granted, granted," broke in Hardman, impatiently poking the fire. "You can't say anything about Germany too severe to suit me. Whatever she needed to keep her from committing the criminal blunder of this war, it is certain that she did not get it. The blunder was made and the price must be paid. But what I say now, as I said at the beginning, is that Latin and Greek are dead languages. For us, for the future, for the competitions of the modern industrial and social era, the classics are no good. For a few ornamental persons a knowledge of them may be a pleasing accomplishment. But they are luxuries, not necessaries. They belong to a bygone age. They have nothing to tell us about the things we most need to know—chemistry and physics, engineering and intensive agriculture, the discovery of new forms and applications of power, the organization of labor and the distribution of wealth, the development of mechanical skill and the increase of production—these are the things that we must study. I say they are the only things that will count for success in the new democracy."

"That is what *you* say," replied Professor De Vries dryly. "But the wisest men of the world have said something very different. No democracy ever has survived, or ever will survive, without an aristocracy at the heart of it. Not an aristocracy of birth and privilege, but one of worth and intelligence; not a band of hereditary lords, but a company of well-chosen leaders. Their value will depend not so much upon their technical knowledge and skill as upon the breadth of their mind, the clearness of their thought, the loftiness of their motives, the balance of their judgment, and the strength of their devotion to duty. For the cultivation of these things I say—pardon the apparent contradiction of what *you* said—I say the study of the classics has been and still is of the greatest value."

"What did George Washington know about the classics?" Hardman interrupted sharply. "He was one of your aristocrats of democracy, I suppose?"

"He was," answered the professor blandly, "and he knew more about the classics than, I fear, you do, my dear Hardman. At all events, he understood what was meant when he was called 'the Cincinnatus of the West'—and he lived up to the ideal, otherwise we should have had no American Republic.

"But let us not drop to personalities. What I maintain is that Latin and Greek are not dead languages, because they still convey living thoughts. The real success of a democracy—the production of a finer manhood—depends less upon mechanics than upon morale. For that the teachings of the classics are excellent. They have a bracing and a steadying quality. They instil a sense of order and they inspire a sense of admiration, both of which are needed by the people—especially the plain people—of a sane democracy. The classics are fresher, younger, more vital and encouraging than most modern books. They have lessons for us to-day—believe me—great words for the present crisis and the pressing duty of the hour."

"Give us an example," said Dick; "something classic to fit this war."

"I have one at hand," responded the professor promptly. He went to the book-shelves and pulled out a small brown volume with a slip of paper in it. He opened the book at the marked place. "It is from the Eighth Satire of Juvenal, beginning at line 79. I will read the Latin first, and afterward a little version which I made the other day."

The old man rolled the lines out in his sonorous voice, almost chanting:

> *"Esto bonus miles, tutor bonus, arbiter idem*
>
> *Integer; ambiguae si quando citabere testis*
>
> *Incertaeque rei, Phalaris licet imperet ut sis*
>
> *Falsus et admoto dictet periuria tauro,*
>
> *Summum crede nefas, animam praeferre pudori*
>
> *Et propter vitam vivendi perdere causas.'"*

"Please to translate, sir," said Dick, copying exactly the professor's classroom phrase and manner.

"To gratify my nephew," said the professor, nodding and winking at Hardman. "But, understand, this is not a real translation. It is only a paraphrase. Here it is:

> *'Be a good soldier, and a guardian just;*
>
> *Likewise an upright judge. Let no one thrust*
>
> *You in a dubious cause to testify,*
>
> *Through fear of tyrant's vengeance, to a lie.*
>
> *Count it a baseness if your soul prefer*
>
> *Safety above what Honor asks of her:*
>
> *And hold it manly life itself to give,*
>
> *Rather than lose the things for which we live.*

It is not half as good as the Latin. But it gives the meaning. How do you like it, Richard?"

"Fine!" answered the young man quickly; "especially the last lines. They are great." He hesitated slightly, and then went on. "Perhaps I ought to tell you now, sir, that I have signed up and got my papers for the training-school at Madison Barracks. I hope you will not be angry with me."

The old man put both hands on the lad's shoulders and looked at him with a suspicious moisture in his eyes. He swallowed hard a couple of times. You could see the big Adam's apple moving up and down in his wrinkled throat.

"Angry!" he cried. "Why, boy, I love you for it."

Hardman, who was a thoroughly good fellow at heart, held out his hand.

"Good for you, Dick! But I must be going now. I am putting up at the Ivy. Will you walk up with me? I'd like to have a word with you."

The two men walked in silence along the shady, moon-flecked streets of the tranquil old university town. Then the elder one spoke.

"You have done the right thing, I am sure. That officers' training-school is a good place to get a practical education. When you are through, how would you like to have a post in the Ordnance Department at Washington? I have some influence there and believe I could get you in without difficulty."

"Thanks, a lot," answered the lad modestly. "You're awfully kind. But, if you don't mind my saying so, I think I'd rather have service at the front—that is, if I can qualify for it."

There was another long silence before Hardman spoke again, with an apparent change of subject:

"I wish you would tell me what you really think of your uncle's views on the classics, you and the other fellows of your age in the university."

Dick hesitated a moment before he replied:

"Well, personally, you know, I believe what Uncle says is usually about right. He has the habit of it. But I allow when he gets on his hobby he rides rather hard. Most of the other fellows have given up the classics—they like the modern-language course with sciences better—perhaps it's softer. They say not; but I know the classics are hard enough. I flunked out on my Greek exam junior year. So, you see, I'm not a very good judge. But, anyhow, wasn't the bit he read us from Juvenal simply fine? And didn't he read it well? I've felt that a hundred times, but never knew how to say it."

It was in the early fall of 1918, more than a year later, that Hardman came once more into the familiar library at Calvinton. He had read the casualty list of the last week of August and came to condole with his friend De Vries.

The old man sat in the twilight of the tranquil book-lined room, leaning back in his armchair, with an open letter on the table before him. He gave his hand cordially to Hardman and thanked him for his sympathetic words. He talked quietly and naturally about Dick, and confessed how much he should miss the boy—as it were, his only son.

"Yes," he said quietly. "I am going to be lonely, but I am not forsaken. I shall be sad sometimes, but never sorry—always proud of my boy. Would you like to see this letter? It is the last that he wrote."

It was a young, simple letter, full of cheerful joking and personal details and words of affection which the shy lad would never have spoken face to face. At the end he wrote:

"Well, dear Governor, this is a rough life, and some parts are not easy to bear. But I want you to know that I was never happier in all my days. I know that we are fighting for a good cause, justice, and freedom, and a world made clean from this beastly German militarism. The things that the Germans have done to France and Belgium must be stopped, and they must never be done again. We want a decent world to live in, and we are going to have it, no matter what it costs. Of course I should like to live through it all, if I can do it with honor. But a man never can tell what is going to happen. And I certainly would rather give up my life than the things we are fighting for—the things you taught me to believe are according to the will of God. So good-night for the present, Uncle, and sleep well.

"Your loving nephew and son,

"DICK."

Hardman's hand shook a little as he laid the paper on the table.

"It is a beautiful letter," he said.

"Yes," nodded the old professor, putting his hand upon it; "it is a classic; very clear and simple and high-minded. The German Crown Prince says our American soldiers do not know what they are fighting for. But Richard knew. It was to defend 'the things for which we live' that he gladly gave his life."

September, 1918.

HALF-TOLD TALES

THE NEW ERA AND CARRY ON

The Commandant of the Marine Hospital was at his desk, working hard, when the door of the room was flung open and the Officer of the Day rushed in.

"Sir," he exploded, "the New Era has come."

"Very likely, Mr. Corker," answered the Commandant. "It has been coming continually since the world began. But is that any reason why you should enter without knocking, and with your coat covered with bread-crumbs and cigarette-ashes?"

So the Officer of the Day went outside, brushed his coat, knocked at the door, and awaited orders.

"Mr. Corker," said the Commandant, "have the kindness to bring me your report on the condition of yesterday's cases, and let me know what operations are indicated for to-day. Good morning. Orderly, my compliments to the Executive Officer, and I wish to see him at once."

When the Executive Officer arrived, he began:

"Sir, the New Era—"

"Quite so, Mr. Greel, but you understand this Hospital has to carry on as required in any kind of an era. How many patients did we receive yesterday? Good. Have we enough bedding and provisions? Bad. Attend to it immediately, and let me know the result of your efforts to remedy a situation which should never have arisen. The Navy cannot be run on hot air."

As the Executive Officer went out he held the door open for the Head Nurse to pass in. She was a fine, upstanding creature, tremulous with emotion.

"Oh, Doctor," she cried, "I simply must tell you about the New Era. Woman Suffrage is going to save the world."

"I hope so, Miss Dooby, it certainly needs saving. Meantime how are things in the pneumonia ward?"

"Two deaths last night, sir, three new cases this morning. Oxygen is running short: no beef-tea or milk. Five of my nurses have gone to attend conventions of woman—"

"Slackers," interrupted the Commandant. "Put them on report for leaving the ship without permission. I shall attend to their cases. Fill their places from the volunteer list. Be so good as to send the head steward here immediately."

"I'm very sorry, Sir," said the steward, "but ye see it's just this way. The mess-boys was holdin' a New Era mass-meetin', and the cook he forgot—"

"Milk and beef-tea!" growled the Commandant as if they were swear-words. "What the devil is this new influenza that has struck the hospital? Steward, you will provide what the head nurse requires at once. Orderly, my cap, and call Mr. Greel to accompany me on inspection."

In the galley the fires were out, the ovens cold, the soup-kettles empty, and all the cooks, dish-washers, and scrubbers were absorbing the eloquence of the third assistant pie-maker, who stood on an empty biscuit-box and explained the glories of the one-hour day in the New Era.

"'Ten*shun!*" yelled the Orderly, and the force of habit brought the men up, stiff and silent. The Commandant looked around the circle, grinning.

"My word!" he cried, "what a beautiful sight! What do you think this is—a blooming debating society? Wrong! It's a hospital, with near a thousand sick and wounded to take care of. And it's going to be done, see? And you're going to help do it, see? No work—no pay and no food! Neglect of orders means extra duty and no liberty—perhaps a couple of twenty-four-hour days in the brig. That's the rule in all eras, see? Now get busy, all of you. Chow at twelve as usual. Carry on, men."

"Aye, aye, sir," they answered cheerily, for they were weary of the third assistant pie-maker's brand of talk and felt the pangs of healthy hunger.

Then came the second engineer, out of breath with running, followed by two or three helpers.

"Fire, captain," he gasped, "fire in the fuel-room—awful blaze—started in the wood box—cigarette—we were just settin' round talkin' over what we were goin' to do in the New Era, an' the first thing we knew it was burnin' like—"

"The New Era," snapped the Commandant, "and be damned to it! Sound the fire-call. All hands to quarters. Lead along the hose. Follow me," he cried, hurrying forward through the gathering smoke, "this ship must be saved."

And so it was—strictly in conformity with the old laws that fire burns, water quenches, and every man must do his duty promptly. On these ancient principles, and others equally venerable, the hospital carried on its good work. But the Commandant made one new rule. It cost five dollars to mention the New Era within its walls.

THE PRIMITIVE AND HIS SANDALS

"I am sick of all this," said the Great Author, sweeping his hand over the silver-laden dinner-table. He seemed to include in his gesture the whole house and the broad estate surrounding it. "It bores me, and I don't believe it can be right."

His wife, at the other end of the table, shining in her low-necked dress with diamonds on her breast and in her hair, leaned forward anxiously, knowing her husband's temperament.

"But, Nicholas," she said, "what do you mean? You have earned all this by your work as a writer. You are the greatest man in the country. You are entitled to a fine house and a large estate."

He gravely nodded his big head with its flamboyant locks, and lit a fresh cigarette.

"Quite right, my dear," said he, "you are always right on practical affairs. But, you see, this is an artistic affair. My books are realistic and radical. They teach the doctrine of the universal level, that no man can be above other men. They have made poverty, perhaps not exactly popular, but at least romantic. My villains are always rich and my heroes poor. The people like this; but it is rather a strain to believe it and keep on believing it. If my work is to hold the public it must have illustrations—moving pictures, you know! Something in character! Nobody else can do that as well as I can. It will be better than many advertisements. I am going to become a virtuous peasant, a son of the soil, a primitive."

His wife laughed, with a slight nervous tremor in her voice. She knew her husband's temperament, to be sure, but she never knew just how far it would carry him.

"I think you must be a little crazy, Nicholas," she said.

"Thank you, Alexandra," he answered, "thank you for the temperate flattery. Evidently you have heard the old proverb about genius and madness. But why not make the compliment complete and say 'absolutely crazy'?"

"Well," she replied, "because I do not understand just what you propose to do. Are you going to impoverish yourself and the whole family? Are you thinking of turning over your farms to these stupid peasants who will let them go to rack and ruin? Will you give your property to the village council who will drink it up in a month? You know how much money Peter needs; he is a member of twelve first-class clubs. And Olga's husband is not earning much. Are you going to starve your children and grandchildren for the sake of an idea of consistency in art?"

The Great Author was now standing in front of the fireplace, warming himself and filling a pipe. The flames behind him made an aureole in his extravagant white hair and beard. He smiled and puffed slowly at his pipe. At last he answered.

"My dear, you go too fast and too far. You know I am enthusiastic, but have you ever known me to be silly? It would be wrong to make you and the children suffer. I have no right to do that."

{Illustration: I am going to become a virtuous peasant, a son of the soil, a primitive}

She nodded her head emphatically, and a look of comprehension spread over her face. "Suppose," he continued, "suppose that I should make over the real estate and farms to you—you are an excellent manager. And suppose that I should put the personal estate, including copyrights, into a trust, the income to be paid to you and the children. You would take care of me while I became a primitive, wouldn't you?"

"I would," she answered, "you know I would. But think how uncomfortable it will be for you. While we are living in luxury, you—"

"Don't worry about that," he interrupted with a laugh. "I shall have all the luxury I want: flannel shirts, loose around the neck, instead of these infernal stiff collars; velveteen trousers and jacket instead of this waiter's uniform; and I shall go barefoot when the weather is suitable—do you understand? Barefoot in the summer grass—it will be immense."

"But your food," she asked, "how will you manage that on a primitive basis?"

"You will manage it," he replied, "you know I have always preferred beefsteak and onions to any French dish. Champagne does not agree with me. I'd rather have a glass of the straight stuff, without any gas in it."

"But your sleeping arrangements," she murmured, "are you going to leave the house? Our bedroom is not exactly primitive."

"No fear of it," he answered. "There is a little room beyond your bathroom. Put an iron cot in there, with a soft mattress, linen sheets, and light blankets. I'll do my morning wash at the pump in the yard, for the sake of the picture. When I want a bath you'll leave the door of the room open if you are not actually in the tub."

"Nicholas," she said, with a Mona Lisa smile, "for an author you have a very clever way of putting things. But suppose we have guests at the house, you can't come to dinner in dirty clothes and with bare feet."

"Certainly not," he answered. "I shall put on clean flannels, clean velveteens, and sandals."

"Sandals," she murmured, "sandals for dinner are simply wonderful. Do you think I could—"

"Not at all, my dear," said the Great Author firmly. "Your present style of dress becomes you amazingly. I am the only one who has to do the primitive."

So the arrangements were completed. The interviewers who came to the house described the Great Author in his loose flannels and velveteens, with bare feet, returning from labor in the fields. The moving pictures were full of him. But the sandals did not appear. There were no flash-lights permitted at the part-primitive dinner-table.

DIANA AND THE LIONS

In the darkest hour before the dawn, Diana floated away from her Garden Tower and came down between the Lions on the Library Steps.

At first, she did not know they were Lions. She thought they were Cats, and so she was afraid. For she was very lightly clad; and (except in Egypt) Cats are terrible to undomesticated goddesses. Diana shivered as she strung her bow for defense. She felt that she was divine, but she knew that she had cold feet.

In truth, the Library Steps were wet and glistening, for there had been a shower after midnight. But now the gibbous moon was giving a silent imitation of an arc-light high in the western heaven. Her beams silver-plated the weird architecture of the shrines of Commerce which face the great Temple dedicated to the Three Muses of New York—Astor, Lenox, and Tilden.

But on the awful animals guarding the steps the light was florid, like a flush of sunburn discovered by the ablution of a warranted complexion cream. They were wonderfully pink, and Diana hastened to draw an arrow from her quiver, for it seemed to her as if her feline neighbors were beginning to glow with rage.

"Do not shoot," said the ruddier one; "we are not angry, we are only blushing." And he glanced at her costume.

Diana was astonished to hear a masculine voice utter such a modest sentiment. But being a woman, she knew that the first word does not count.

"Cats never blush," she answered boldly, "no matter how big they are."

"But we are not Cats," they cried, ramping suddenly like crests on a millionaire's note-paper. "We are Lions!"

Diana smiled at this, for now she felt safe, remembering that when a male begins to boast he is not dangerous.

"Roar a little for me, please," she said, laying down her unconcealed weapon.

"Impossible," said the Northern Lion, "a city ordinance forbids unnecessary noise."

"Nonsense!" interrupted the Southern Lion. "Who would not break a law to oblige a lady?"

"Let us compromise," said the Northern Lion, "and give her our reproduction of an automobile horn."

"No," said the Southern Lion, "we will give her our automatic record of a Book-Advertisement; it is louder."

Then Diana trembled, indeed. But she bravely continued smiling, and said: "Thank you a thousand times for doing it once! And now please tell me what kind of Lions you are."

"Literary Lions," was their prompt and unanimous reply.

"Ah," she cried, clapping her hands with a charming gesture, "how glad I am to meet you! I have been in New York more than twenty years and never seen any one like you before! Come and sit beside me and talk."

The Lions looked at each other rather sheepishly, and glanced up and down the street, as if fearing the approach of a city ordinance. But there was no one in sight except Diana, so they shook their literary locks into a becoming disorder and sat on the steps with her, purring gently.

"Now tell me," she said, "who you are."

If she had been less beautiful they would have resented this. But, as it was, they looked sorry, and asked her if she had never read "Who's Who in America"? She shook her head, and admitted that she had not read it all through.

"Well," said her neighbor on the south, "this is rather an offhand *soiree*, and we may as well cut out proper names. But I will put you wise to the fact that I am the Magazine Lion. I got away from Roosevelt in Africa. He called me 'Mucky,' and I made tracks. Here he cannot hurt me, for they will never let that man do anything in good old New York, not even touch a Tiger."

"And I," said her neighbor on the north, "I am the Academic Lion, of whom you must have heard. My character is noted for its concealed sweetness, and my style leaves nothing to be hoped for. I am literally a man of letters, for I have seventeen degrees. Usually I look literary-lean and nobly dissatisfied, but yesterday I swallowed a British Female Novelist by accident, and that accounts for my inartistic air of cheerfulness. I won my splendid reputation by telling other Lions how they ought to have done their little tricks. But now, tired of that, I have gone into politics. This is my first public office."

Diana was somewhat confused and benumbed by these personally conducted biographies, but she was too well-bred not to appear interested.

"How lovely," she murmured, "to sit between two such Great Personages! I wonder what brought poor little Me to such an honor. And, by the way, how do you happen to be just here? What is this beautiful building behind you? Is it your Palace?"

"It is a Library," said the Academic Lion, with a superior tone.

"The biggest book-heap in America," said the Magazine Lion in his vivid way. "We have them all beaten to a finish—except the old junk-shop down in Washington."

"You forget Boston," said the Academic Lion.

"Who wouldn't?" growled the Magazine Lion.

"Do you mean to tell me," asked Diana, with her most engaging and sprightly air, "that this splendid place is a Library, all full of books, and that you are its most prominent figures, its figureheads, so to speak? How interesting! I have travelled a great deal—under the name of Pasht or Bast, in Egypt, where the Cats liked me; and under the name of Artemis in Greece; and under my own name in Italy. Believe me, I have seen all things that the moon shines upon. But I do not remember having seen Lions on a Library before. How original! How appropriate! How suggestive! But what does it suggest? What are you here for?"

"For educational purposes," said the Academic Lion.

"To catch the eye," said the Magazine Lion, "same as head-lines in a newspaper."

"I see," exclaimed Diana. "You are here to keep the people from getting at the books? How modern!"

This remark made the Academic Lion look like a Sphinx, as if he knew something but did not want to tell. But the Magazine Lion was distinctly flattered.

"Right you are," said he cheerfully, "or next door to it. We don't propose to keep the people out, only the authors. Why, when this place was publicly opened there was not a single author in the exhibit, except John Bigelow."

"Why did you not keep him out?" asked Diana.

"We were not on the spot, then," said the Lion. "Besides, there are some things that even a Lion does not dare to do."

"But I do not understand," said Diana, "precisely why authors should be kept away from a library."

The Magazine Lion laughed. "Silly little thing!" he said, with a fascinating tone of virile condescension. "An author's business is to write books, not to read them. If he reads, he grows intelligent and thoughtful and careful about his work. Those old books spoil him for the modern market. But if he just goes ahead and writes whatever comes into his head, he can do it with a bang, and everybody sits up and pays attention. That's the only way to be original. See?"

"Excuse me," broke in the Academic Lion, "but you go too far, brother. Authors should be encouraged to read, but only under critical guidance and professorial direction. Otherwise they will not be able to classify the books, and tabulate their writers, and know which ones to admire and praise. How can you expect a mere author to comprehend the faulty method of Shakespeare, or the ethical commonplaceness of Dickens and Thackeray, or the vital Ibsenism of Bernard Shaw and the other near-Ibsens, without assistance?"

"But the other people," asked Diana, "what is going to happen to them if you let them go in free and browse among the books?"

"They are less important," answered the Academic Lion. "Besides we expect soon to establish a cranial, neurological, and psychopathic examination which will determine the subliminal, temperamental needs of every applicant. Then we classify the readers in groups, and the books in lists, and the whole thing works with automatic precision."

"And I am going to make the book-lists!" said the Magazine Lion, ecstatically wagging his tail, and half-unconsciously putting his paw around the lady's waist in a spirit of pure comradeship.

But she gently slipped away, stood up, and gracefully covered a yawn with her hand.

"I am ever so much obliged to you Literary Lions for not eating me," said she. "Probably I should have disagreed with you even more than your conversation has with me. I am quite sleepy. And the moon has almost disappeared. I must be going where I can bid it good night."

So Diana rose, with shining limbs, above the housetops, and vanished toward her Garden Tower. The Lions looked disconcerted. "Old-fashioned, Victorian prude!" said one, "Brazen hussy!" said the other. And they climbed back on their Pedestals, resuming their supercilious expression. There I suppose they will stay, no matter what Diana may think of them.

THE HERO AND TIN SOLDIERS

On December twenty-fifth, 1918, that little white house in the park was certainly the happiest dwelling in Calvinton. It was simply running over with Christmas.

You see, there had come to it a most wonderful present, a surprise full of tears and laughter. Captain Walter Mayne reached home on Christmas Eve.

For a while they had thought that he would never come back at all. News had been received that he was grievously wounded in France—shot to pieces, in effect, leading his men near Chateau-Thierry. His life hung on the ragged edge of those wounds. But his wife Katharine always believed that he would pull through. So he did. But he was lacking a leg, his right arm was knocked out of commission for the present, and various other *souvenirs de la grande guerre* were inscribed upon his body.

Then word arrived that he was coming on a transport, with other wounded, to be patched up in a hospital on Staten Island. So his wife Katharine smiled her way through innumerable entanglements of red tape and went to nurse him. Then she set her steady hand to pull all the wires necessary to get him discharged and sent home. Christmas was in her heart and she would not be denied. So it came to pass that the one-legged Hero was in his own house on the happy day, and joy was bubbling all around him.

When the old Pastor entered, late in the afternoon, the Christmas-tree was twinkling with lights, the children swarming and buzzing all over the place, so that he was dazed for a moment. There were Walter's mother and his aunt and his sisters-in-law, boys and girls of various sizes, and a jubilant and entrancing baby. The Pastor took it all in, and was glad of it, but his mind was on the Hero.

Katharine, who always understood everything, whispered softly: "Walter is waiting to see you, Doctor. He is in his study, just across the hall."

Waiting? Well, what can a man whose right leg has been cut off above the knee, and who has not yet been able to get an artificial one—what can he do but wait?

The room was rather dimly lighted; brilliance is not good for the eyes of the wounded. Walter was in a long chair in the corner; his face was bronzed, drawn and lined a little by suffering; but steady and cheerful as ever, with the eager look which had made his students listen to him when he talked to them about English literature.

"My dear Walter," said the Pastor, "my dear boy, we are so glad to have you home with us again. We are very proud of you. You are our Hero."

"Thank you," said Walter, "it is mighty good to be home again. But there is no hero business about it. I only did what all the other Americans who went over there did—fought my—excuse me, my best, against the beastly Germans."

"But your leg," said the Pastor impulsively, "it is gone. Aren't you angry about that?"

Walter was silent for a moment. Then he answered.

"No, I don't think angry is the right word. You remember that story about Nathan Hale in the Revolution—'I only regret that I have but one life to give to my country.' Well, I'm glad that I had two legs to give for my country, and particularly glad that she only needed one of them."

"Tell me a bit about the fighting," said the Pastor, "I want to know what it was like—the hero-touch—you understand?"

"Not for me," said Walter, "and certainly not now. Later on I can tell you something, perhaps. But this is Christmas Day. And war? Well, Doctor, believe me, war is a horrible thing, full of grime and pain, madness, agony, hell—a thing that ought not to be. I have fought alongside of the other fellows to put an end to it, and now—"

The door swung open, and Sammy, the eldest son of the house, pranced in.

"Look, Daddy," he cried, "see what Aunt Emily has sent me for Christmas—a big box of tin soldiers!"

Mayne smiled as the little boy carefully laid the box on his knee; but there was a shadow of pain in his eyes, and he closed them for a few seconds, as if his mind were going back, somewhere, far away. Then he spoke, tenderly, but with a grave voice.

"That's fine, sonny—all those tin soldiers. But don't you think they ought to belong to me? You have lots of other toys, you know. Would you give the soldiers to me?"

The child looked up at him, puzzled for a moment; then a flash of comprehension passed over his face, and he nodded valiantly.

"Sure, Father," he said, "You're the Captain. Keep the soldiers. I'll play with the other toys," and he skipped out of the room.

Mayne's look followed him with love. Then he turned to the old Pastor and a strange expression came into his face, half whimsical and half grim.

"Doctor," he said, "will you do me a favor? Poke up that fire till it blazes. That's right. Now lay this box in the hottest part of the flames. That's right. It will soon be gone."

The elder man did what was asked, with an air of slight bewilderment, as one humors the fancies of an invalid. He wondered whether Mayne's fever had quite left him. He watched the fire bulging the lid and catching round the edges of the box. Then he heard Mayne's voice behind him, speaking very quietly.

"If ever I find my little boy *playing with tin soldiers,* I shall spank him well. No, that wouldn't be quite fair, would it? But I shall tell him why he must not do it, and *I shall make him understand that it's an impossible thing.*"

Then the old Pastor comprehended. There was no touch of fever. The one-legged Hero had come home from the wars completely well and sound in mind. So the two men sat together in love by the Christmas fire, and saw the tin soldiers melt away.

SALVAGE POINT

The Hermanns built their house at the very end of the island, five or six miles from the more or less violently rustic "summer-cottages" which adorned the hills and bluffs around the native village of Winterport.

There was a long point running out to the southward at the mouth of the great bay, rough and rocky for the most part, with little woods of pointed firs on it, some acres of pasture, and a few pockets of fertile soil lying between the stony ridges. A yellow farmhouse, with a red barn beside it, had nestled for near a hundred years in one of these hollows, buying shelter from the winter winds at the cost of an outlook over sea and shore.

It was a large price to pay. The view from the summit of the little hill a few hundred yards away was superb—a wonder even on that wonderful coast of Maine where mountain and sea meet together, forest and flood kiss each other.

But I suppose the old Yankee farmer knew what he wanted when he paid the price and snuggled his house in the hollow. I am certain the Hermanns knew what they wanted when they bought the whole point and perched their house on the very top of the hill, where all the winds of heaven might visit it as roughly as they pleased, but where nothing could rob the outlook of its ever-changing splendor and mystery, its fluent wonder and abiding charm.

You see, the Hermanns knew what they wanted because they had come through a lot of trouble. I met them when they were young—no matter how many years ago—when they were in the thick of it.

Alice Mackaye and Will Hermann had the rare luck to fall in love—a very real and great love—when they were in their early twenties. You would think that extraordinary piece of good fortune would have been enough to set them up for life, wouldn't you? But no. There was an Obstacle. And that Obstacle came very near wrecking them both.

Will Hermann was an artist and the son of an artist. The love of beauty ran in his blood. Otherwise he was poor. He earned a decent living by his painting, but each year's living depended on each year's work. Hence he was in the proletarian class.

Alice Mackaye, on the other hand, belonged to the capitalist class. I say "belonged," because that is precisely the word to describe her situation. Her father was a millionaire sugar-merchant, who lived in an ugly palace near Morristown, New Jersey, and was accustomed to have his own way in that and other States. He was the Obstacle.

He was a florid, handsome old Scotchman, orthodox in religion, shrewd in business, correct in conduct, but with no more sentiment than a hard-shell crab, and obstinate as the devil. His fixed idea was that none of his daughters should ever be carried off by a fortune-hunter. The two older girls apparently escaped this danger by making fairly wealthy matches. But Alice—come away! why should she take up with this impecunious painter? He was good-looking and had the gift of the gab, but what was that worth? If he would come into the sugar-business, where a place was waiting for him, and make good there, it would be all right. Otherwise, the affair must be broken off, absolutely, finally, and forever. From this you can see that the Obstacle was not bad-hearted, but only pig-headed.

Well, for five or six years things drifted rather miserably along this way. Will Hermann was forbidden the house at Morristown. Alice was practically a captive; her correspondence was censored. But of course, even before Marconi, wireless communication in matters of this kind has always been possible.

The trouble was that the state of affairs between them, while conventionally correct, was thoroughly unnatural and full of peril. Alice, a very good girl, obedient and tractable, was in danger of becoming a recalcitrant and sour old maid. Will, a healthy and normal young man, with no bad habits, was in danger of being driven to them by the emptiness and exasperation of his mind. The worst of it all was that both of the young people were, in accordance with a well-known law of nature, growing older with what seemed to them a frightful and unreasonable rapidity. The years crawled like snails. But the sum of them rose by leaps and bounds to an appalling total. Alice found two grey hairs in her red-gold locks. Will had to use glasses for reading fine print at night. From their point of view, decrepitude, senility, dotage stared them in the face, while the bright voyage of life which they were resolved to make only together, was threatened with shipwreck among the shoals of interminable delay.

It was at this juncture of affairs that they came to me, as fine-looking a young couple as ever I saw. They were good, as mortals go; they were loyal and upright, they wanted no scandal, no rumpus in the family, no trouble or pain for anybody else; but they wanted to belong to each other much more than they wanted to belong to any class, artistic, proletarian, or capitalist. And they were desperate because of the pertinacity of the Obstacle, whom they both respected fully as much as he deserved.

When they had stated their case, I made my answer.

"So far as I can see, the salvage of your ship of love depends entirely on yourselves. Mr. Hermann is not after a fortune, he only wants his girl; is that so? {Hermann nodded vigorously.} And Miss Mackaye does not care about being supported in the manner of living to which she has been accustomed; she only wants to live with the man whom she has chosen; is that so? {Alice blushed and nodded.} Well, then, why shouldn't you lay your course and sail ahead together? You are both of age, aren't you?"

They smiled at each other. "Yes, and a little over."

"But my father!" said Alice. "You know I honor him, and I can never deny his authority over me."

Here was the turn of the talk, the critical moment, the point where the chosen counsellor had to fall back upon the ultimate reality of his faith.

"Well," I said, "you are absolutely correct, dear daughter, in your feeling toward your father. He has earned his money and has a right to dispose of it as he will. But, you know, there is a statute of limitations in regard to the authority of parents over the *lives* of their children. You have passed the limitation. What do you want to do?"

"To be married to Will Hermann," she said, "for better for worse, for richer for poorer, I don't care. But I don't want a family quarrel, a runaway match, all that horrid newspaper talk." Here she was evidently a little excited and on the verge of tears.

"Certainly not," I hastened to reassure her, "you can't possibly have a runaway match, because there is nothing for you to run away from. There is not a single duty in your father's house which you have not fulfilled, and of which your sisters can not now relieve you. There is no authority in the world which has the right to command the sacrifice of your life to another's judgment. There is only one thing that stands in your way, and that is your claim on a large inheritance. I understand you are quite willing to let that go. You are not even 'running away' from it—that is not the word—you are ready to *jettison* it."

She looked puzzled, and murmured; "I don't exactly understand what that means."

"To jettison," I said, in that learned and dispassionate manner which is sometimes useful in relieving an emotional situation, "is a seafaring phrase. It means throwing overboard a part or the whole of a cargo in order to save the ship. As far as I can see that is the question which is up to you and your best friend at the present moment. Are you prepared to jettison the claim on a big fortune for the sake of making your voyage of life together?"

They looked at each other and a kind of radiance spread over their faces. "Surely," they answered with one voice. "But how can the marriage be arranged," asked Alice, "without a row in the family?"

"Very easily," I answered. "Both of you are over age, though you don't look it. Our good lawyer friend Harrison will help you to get the license. Fix your day for the wedding, neither secret nor notorious; invite anybody you like, and come to me on the day you have chosen. The arrangements will be made. You shall be married, all right."

So they came, and I married them, and it was a very good job.

They had some years of difficulty and uncertainty during which I caught brief glimpses of them now and then, always cheerful and happy together. In the course of time the Obstacle, being not at all bad-hearted but only pig-headed, probably relented a little, and finally was gathered to his fathers, according to the common lot of man. The older sisters behaved very well about the inheritance, and Alice was not left portionless. She brought three fine boys into the world. The house on Salvage Point was built by her and Will together.

It was there that I spent a day with them, in the summer of 1918, after many years during which we had not met. I was on naval duty, with Commander Kidd, of a certain station on the Maine coast. By invitation we put in with the motorboat S.P. 297, at Salvage Point. So it was that I met my old friends again, and knew what had become of their barque of love which I had helped to save from shipwreck.

The house on the peak of the hill was just what it ought to be; not aggressively rustic, not obtrusively classic—white pillars in front of it, and a terrace, but nothing dominating—it had the air of a very large and habitable lighthouse.

The extraordinary thing was the arrangement of the grounds. At every point one came upon some reminder of salvage. On the glorious August day when I was there, shipwreck seemed impossible: the Southern Way which opened to the Ocean was dancing with gay waves; the blue mountains of Maine were tranquil on the horizon.

"But you see," said Will Hermann, "this is really rather a dangerous point, though it is so beautiful. It is the gateway of the open sea, and there are three big ledges across it. A ship that has lost her bearings a little, or is driving in through thick weather, easily comes to grief. But there is not often a loss of life, only the ship goes to pieces. And we save the pieces."

It was true. There was a terrace west of the house, with a balustrade made of the taffrail of a wrecked brigantine. The gateway to the garden was the door of an old wheel-house. There was a pergola constructed from the timbers of a four-masted schooner that had broken up on the third ledge. The bow of the sloop *Christabel*, with the name still painted on it, was just outside the garden-gate. Everywhere you saw old anchor-bits, and rudder-posts, and knees, all silver-greyed by the weather, and fitted in to the *decor* of the place.

The prettiest thing of all was a crow's-nest from a wrecked brigantine, perched on the highest point of the hill, and looking out over the marvellous panorama of sea and shore, island and mountain. Here we sat, after a hearty luncheon with Alice and her three boys and half-a-dozen others who were with them in a kind of summer camp-school; and while we smoked our pipes, Will Hermann told this story.

"You see, Alice and I have a mania for things that have been salvaged. We don't like the idea of the wrecks, of course. But they would happen any way, whether we were here or not. And since that is so, we like to live here on the point and help save what we can. Sometimes we get a chance to do something for the crews of the little ships that come ashore—hot supper and dry clothes and so forth. But the most interesting salvage case that we ever had on the point was one in which there was really no wreck at all.

"It was a bright September afternoon ten years ago—one of those silver-blue days when there is a little quivering haze in the air everywhere, but no fog. We were sitting up here and looking out to sea. Just beyond the end of Dunker Rock a large motor-boat came in sight through the haze. She was about sixty feet long, with a low cabin forward, a cockpit aft, and a raised place for the steersman amidship—a good-looking craft, and evidently very speedy. She carried no flag or pennant. She came driving on, full tilt, straight toward us. We supposed of course she would turn east through the narrow channel to Winterport, or sheer off to the west into the Southern Way and go up the bay. But not a point did she swerve. Steady on she came, toward the three big ledges that lie out there beyond that bit of shingly beach at the end of the point.

"'I can't see any helmsman,' said Alice, 'those people must be asleep or crazy. Give them a hail through the megaphone. Perhaps you can make them hear.'

"So I yelled at the top of my lungs, and Alice waved her jersey. We might as well have hailed a comet. That boat ran straight for the ledges as if she meant to hurdle them. She came near doing it, too. Over the first she scraped, as if her heel had hit it. Over the second she shivered, hanging there for a second till a wave lifted her. On the third she bumped hard and checked her way for a moment, but the engine kept going, and finally she got herself over somehow and ran head on to the beach.

"Of course we were excited, and everybody hurried down to see what this crazy performance meant. There was not a creature on the boat, alive or dead.

"Everything was shipshape. The little craft had evidently been used for fishing. There were rough men's clothes on board, rubber boots and oilskins, fresh water and provisions, blankets in the cabin, fishing-lines and bait in the cockpit, gasolene in the tanks—a nice little outfit, all complete, and no one to run it.

"Where had she come from? There were no names on bow or stern, no papers in the cabin. Who had started her on this crazy voyage? How did she get away from them? Had they perhaps abandoned her and cast her adrift for some mysterious reason? Undoubtedly there were men—apparently three—on board when she set out. What had happened to them? A drunken quarrel? Or possibly one of the men had fallen overboard; the others had jumped in to save him; the engine had started up and the boat left them all in the lurch. Perhaps one or all of them may have had some reason for wanting to 'disappear without a trace,' so they hit upon the plan of going ashore at some lonely place and turning the boat loose to wreck herself. That would have been a stupid scheme of course, but not too stupid to be human.

"It was just a little piece of sea mystery to which we had no clew. So we debated it for an hour, and then set about the more important work of salvaging the stranded derelict. Fortunately she went ashore near the last of the ebb, and now lay comfortably in the mud, apparently little damaged except for some long scratches on her side, and a broken blade in her propeller. We dug away the mud at bow and stern, made fast a tow-line, and when the tide came in my small cruiser pulled her off easily. In the morning the mysterious stranger lay at anchor in the cove round the corner, as quiet as a China duck.

"Of course we advertised in the coast newspapers, giving a description of the boat—'came ashore,' etc.

"Three days later a boy about thirteen years old turned up at Winterport. He came from a village at the northeast corner of the bay forty miles away. He guessed the boat was his father's, but couldn't say for sure until he had seen it. So he came down to the point and identified it beyond a doubt. He told his story very simply.

"The boat belonged to his father, who was a widow-man with only one child. He used the boat for fishing, and sometimes he took Johnny with him, sometimes not. On the trips without the boy he used to stay out longer, sometimes a week or ten days. About a week ago he had started out on one of these trips with two other men. They had a dory in tow. They hadn't come back. Johnny had seen the piece in the paper. Here was the boat, for sure, but no dory. As for the rest of the story—well, that was all that Johnny had to tell us about it—the mystery was as far away as ever.

"He was a fine, sturdy little chap, with tanned face and clear blue eyes. He was rather shaken by his experience, of course, but he wouldn't cry—not for the world. We were glad to take him in for the night, while we verified his story by telegraph. It seemed the boat was practically his only inheritance, and the first question he asked, after we had gone over it, was how much we wanted him to pay for salvage.

"'Just one cent,' said Alice, taking the words out of my mouth, 'and what is more, we are going to have her repaired for you. She isn't much hurt.' So the boy stammered out the best kind of a 'thank you' that he could manage, and the look in his eyes made up for the lack of words. That was the time that he came nearest to crying. But Alice saved him by asking what he was going to do with the boat.

"He had an idea that he could run her himself, perhaps with another man to help him, for fishing in the fall, and for pleasure parties in the summer. He didn't want to cut loose from home altogether and sell the boat. Perhaps Dad might come back, some day, or send a letter. Anyway Johnny wanted to stay by a seafaring life.

"So we arranged the repairs and all that, and got a man to help on the homeward trip, and after a few days Johnny sailed off with his patrimony. That is what Alice and I consider our neatest job of salvage."

"Did it work all right?" I asked.

"Finely," said Will Hermann, "like a charm."

"And where is the lad now?"

"Bo'sun's mate on a certain destroyer somewhere off the coast of France, fighting in the U. S. Navee."

"And the father?" I inquired, being one of those old-fashioned persons who like all the loose ends of a story to be tied up. "Was anything ever heard of him?"

"That," answered my friend, carefully shaking out the ashes of his pipe beyond the crow's-nest rail, "that belongs in a different compartment of the ship."

THE BOY OF NAZARETH DREAMS

There was a Boy in Nazareth long ago whose after-life was wonderful, and whose story is written in the heart of mankind. His birth was predicted in dreams foretelling marvellous things of him, and in later years there were many true visions wherein he played a wondrous part.

Did he not also dream, in the days of his youth, while he was growing in wisdom and stature, and in favor with God and man? It would be strange indeed if his boyhood was not often visited and illumined by those swift flashes of insight and clear unveilings of hidden things, which we call dreams but which are in truth rays from "the fountain light of all our day."

The first journey that he made, his earliest visit to a great city, the three days and nights when he was lost there—surely these were times when visions must have come to him, full of mystery and wonder, yet clothed in the simple, real forms of this world, which he was learning to know. So I let my revery follow him on that unrecorded path, remembering where it led him, and imagining, in the form of dreams, what may have met him on his way.

I. THE JOURNEY TO THE CITY

There was not a lad in the country town of Nazareth, nestled high on the bosom of the Galilean hills, who did not often look eagerly southward over the plain toward the dark mountains of Samaria, and think of the great city which lay beyond them, and long for the time when he would be old enough to go with his family on pilgrimage to Jerusalem.

That journey would carry him out of childhood. It would mark the beginning of his life as a "son of the commandment," a member of the Hebrew nation. Moreover it would be an adventure—a very great and joyous adventure, which youth loves.

Palestine, in the days when Augustus Caesar was Lord of the World, was an exciting country to travel in. It was full of rovers and soldiers of fortune from many lands. It was troubled by mobs and tumults and rebellions, infested with landlopers and brigands. Jerusalem itself was not only a great city, it was a boisterous and boiling city, crowded with visitors from all parts of the world, merchants and travellers, princes and beggars, citizens of Rome and children of the Desert. There were strange sights to be seen there, and all kinds of things were sold in the markets. So while the heart of young Nazareth longed for it, the heart of older Nazareth was not without anxieties and apprehensions in regard to the first pilgrimage.

This was doubly true in the home of the Boy of whom I speak. He was the first-born, the darling of his parents, a lad beloved by all who knew him. His mother hung on him with mystical joy and hope. He was the apple of her eye. Deep in her soul she kept the memory of angelic words which had come to her while she carried him under her heart—words which made her believe that her son would be the morning-star of Israel and a light unto the Gentiles. So she cherished the Boy and watched over him with tender, unfailing care, as her most precious possession, her living, breathing, growing treasure.

When he reached the age of twelve, he was old enough to go up to the Temple and take part in the national feast of the Passover. So she clad him in the garments of youth and made him ready for the four days' pilgrimage.

It was a camping-trip, a wonder-walk, full of variety, with a spice of danger and a feast of delight.

The Boy was the joy of the journey. His keen interest in all things seen and heard was like a refreshing spring of water to the older pilgrims. They had so often travelled the same road that they had forgotten that it might be new every morning. His unwearying vigor and gladness as he ran down the hillsides, or scrambled among the rocks far above the path, or roamed through the fields filling his hands with flowers, was like a merry song that cheered the long miles of the way. He was glad to be alive, and it made the others glad to look at him.

There were sixty or seventy kinsfolk and neighbors, plain rustic men and women, in the little company that set out from Nazareth. The men carried arms to protect the caravan from robbers or marauders. As they wound slowly down the steep, stony road to the plain of Esdraelon the Boy ran ahead, making short cuts, turning aside to find a partridge's nest among the bushes, jumping from rock to rock like a young gazelle, or poising on the edge of some cliff in sheer delight of his own sure-footedness.

His body was outlined against the sky; his blue eyes (like those of his mother, who was a maid of Bethlehem) sparkled with the joy of living; his long hair was lifted and tossed by the wind of April. But his mother's look followed him anxiously, and her heart often leaped in her throat.

"My son," she said, as they took their noon-meal in the valley at the foot of dark Mount Gilboa, "you must be more careful. Your feet might slip."

"Mother," answered the Boy, "I am truly very careful. I always put my feet in the places that God has made for them—on the big, strong rocks that will not roll. It is only because I am so happy that you think I am careless."

The tents were pitched, the first night, under the walls of Bethshan, a fortified city of the Romans. Set on a knoll above the river Jordan, the town loomed big and threatening over the little camp of the Galilean pilgrims. But they kept aloof from it, because it was a city of the heathen. Its theatres and temples and palaces were accursed. The tents were indifferent to the city, and when the night opened its star-fields above them and the heavenly lights rose over the mountains of Moab and Samaria, the Boy's clear voice joined in the slumber-song of the pilgrims:

> *"I will lift up mine eyes to the hills,*
>
> *From whence cometh my help;*
>
> *My help cometh from the Lord,*
>
> *Who made heaven and earth.*
>
> *He will not suffer thy foot to stumble,*
>
> *He who keepeth thee will not slumber.*
>
> *Behold, He who guardeth Israel*
>
> *Will neither slumber nor sleep."*

Then they drew their woollen cloaks over their heads and rested on the ground in peace.

For two days their way led through the wide valley of the Jordan, along the level land that stretched from the mountains on either side to the rough gulch where the river was raging through its jungle. They passed through broad fields of ripe barley and ripening wheat, where the quail scuttled and piped among the thick-growing stalks. There were fruit-orchards and olive-groves on the foothills, and clear streams ran murmuring down through glistening oleander thickets. Wild flowers sprang in every untilled corner; tall spikes of hollyhocks, scarlet and blue anemones, clusters of mignonette, rock-roses, and cyclamens, purple iris in the moist places, and many-colored spathes of gladiolus growing plentifully among the wheat.

The larks sang themselves into the sky in the early morn. Hotter grew the sun and heavier the air in that long trough below the level of the sea. The song of birds melted away. Only the hawks wheeled on motionless wings above silent fields, watching for the young quail or the little rabbits, hidden among the grain.

The pilgrims plodded on in the heat. Companies of soldiers with glittering arms, merchants with laden mules jingling their bells, groups of ragged thieves and bold beggars met and jostled the peaceful travellers on the road. Once a little band of robbers, riding across the valley to the land of Moab, turned from a distance toward the Nazarenes, circled swiftly around them like hawks, whistling and calling shrilly to one another. But there was small booty in that country caravan, and the men who guarded it looked strong and tough; so the robbers whirled away as swiftly as they had come.

The Boy had stood close to his father in this moment of danger, looking on with surprise at the actions of the horsemen.

"What did those riders want?" he asked.

"All we have," answered the man.

"But it is very little," said the Boy. "Nothing but our clothes and some food for our journey. If they were hungry, why did they not ask of us?"

The man laughed. "These are not the kind that ask," he said, "they are the kind that take—what they will and when they can."

"I do not like them," said the Boy. "Their horses were beautiful, but their faces were hateful—like a jackal that I saw—in the gulley behind Nazareth one night. His eyes were burning red as fire. Those men had fires inside of them."

For the rest of that afternoon he walked more quietly and with thoughtful looks, as if he were pondering the case of men who looked like jackals and had flames within them.

At sunset, when the camp was made outside the gates of the new city of Archelaus, on a hillock among the corn-fields, he came to his mother with his hands full of the long lavender and rose and pale-blue spathes of the gladiolus-lilies.

"Look, mother," he cried, "are they not fine—like the clothes of a king?"

"What do you know of kings?" she answered, smiling. "These are only wild lilies of the field. But a great king, like Solomon, has robes of thick silk, and jewels on his neck and his fingers, and a big crown of gold on his head."

"But that must be very heavy," said the Boy, tossing his head lightly. "It must tire him to wear a crown-thing and such thick robes. Besides, I think the lilies are really prettier. They look just as if they were glad to grow in the field."

The third night they camped among the palm-groves and heavy-odored gardens of Jericho, where Herod's splendid palace rose above the trees. The fourth day they climbed the wild, steep, robber-haunted road from the Jordan valley to the highlands of Judea, and so came at sundown to their camp-ground among friends and neighbors on the closely tented slope of the Mount of Olives, over against Jerusalem.

What an evening that was for the Boy! His first sight of the holy city, the city of the great king, the city lifted up and exalted on the sides of the north, beautiful for situation, the joy of the whole earth! He had dreamed of her glory as he listened at his mother's knee to the wonder-tales of David and Solomon and the brave adventures of the fighting Maccabees. He had prayed for the peace of Jerusalem every night as he kneeled by his bed and lifted his hands toward the holy place. He had tried a thousand times to picture her strength and her splendor, her marvels and mysteries, her multitude of houses and her vast bulwarks, as he strayed among the humble cottages of Nazareth or sat in the low doorway of his own home.

Now his dream had come true. He looked into the face of Jerusalem, just across the deep, narrow valley of the Kidron, where the shadows of the evening were rising among the tombs. The huge battlemented walls, encircling the double mounts of Zion and Moriah—the vast huddle of white houses, covering hill and hollow with their flat roofs and standing so close together that the streets were hidden among them—the towers, the colonnades, the terraces—the dark bulk of the Roman castle—the marble pillars and glittering roof of the Temple in its broad court on the hilltop—it was a city of stone and ivory and gold, rising clear against the soft saffron and rose and violet of the sunset sky.

The Boy sat with his mother on the hillside while the light waned, and the lamps began to twinkle in the city, the stars to glow in the deepening blue. He questioned her eagerly—what is that black tower?—why does the big roof shine so bright?—where was King David's house?—where are we going to-morrow?

"To-morrow," she answered, "you will see. But now it is the sleep-time. Let us sing the psalm that we used to sing at night in Nazareth—but very softly, not to disturb the others—for you know this psalm is not one of the songs of the pilgrimage."

So the mother and her Child sang together with low voices:

"In peace will I both lay me down and sleep,

For thou, Lord, makest me dwell in safety."

The tune and the words quieted the Boy. It was like a bit of home in a far land.

II. THE GILDED TEMPLE

The next day was full of wonder and excitement. It was the first day of the Feast, and the myriad of pilgrims crowded through the gates and streets of the city, all straining toward the enclosure of the Temple, within whose walls two hundred thousand people could be gathered. On every side the Boy saw new and strange things: soldiers in their armor, and shops full of costly wares; richly dressed Sadducees with their servants following; Jews from far-away countries, and curious visitors from all parts of the world; ragged children of the city, and painted women of the street, and beggars and outcasts of the lower quarters, and rich ladies with their retinues, and priests in their snowy robes.

The family from Nazareth passed slowly through the confusion, and the Boy, bewildered by the changing scene, longed to get to the Temple. He thought everything must be quiet and holy there. But when they came into the immense outer court, with its porticos and alcoves, he found the confusion worse than ever. For there the money-changers and the buyers and sellers of animals for sacrifice were bargaining and haggling; and the thousands of people were jostling and pushing one another; and the followers of the Pharisees and the Sadducees were disputing; and on many faces he saw that strange look which speaks of a fire in the heart, so that it seemed like a meeting-place of robbers.

His father had bought a lamb for the Passover sacrifice, at one of the stalls in the outer court, and was carrying it on his shoulder. He pressed on through the crowd at the Beautiful Gate, the Boy and his mother following until they came to the Court of the Women. Here the mother stayed, for that was the law—a woman must not go farther. But the Boy was now "a son of the Commandment," and he followed his father through the Court of Israel to the entrance of the Court of the Priests. There the little lamb was given to a priest, who carried it away to the great stone altar in the middle of the court.

The Boy could not see what happened then, for the place was crowded and busy. But he heard the blowing of trumpets, and the clashing of cymbals, and the chanting of psalms. Black clouds of smoke went up from the hidden altar; the floor around was splashed and streaked with red. After a long while, as it seemed, the priest brought back the dead body of the lamb, prepared for the Passover supper.

"Is this our little lamb?" asked the Boy as his father took it again upon his shoulder.

The father nodded.

"It was a very pretty one," said the Boy. "Did it have to die?"

The father looked down at him curiously. "Surely," he said, "it had to be offered on the altar, so that we can keep our feast according to the law of Moses to-night."

"But why," persisted the Boy, "must all the lambs be killed in the Temple? Does God like that? How many do you suppose were brought to the altar to-day?"

"Tens of thousands," answered the father.

"It is a great many," said the Boy, sighing. "I wish one was enough."

He was silent and thoughtful as they made their way through the Court of the Women and found the mother and went back to the camp on the hillside. That night the family ate their Paschal feast, with their loins girded as if they were going on a journey, in memory of the long-ago flight of the Israelites from Egypt. There was the roasted lamb, with bitter herbs, and flat cakes of bread made without yeast. A cup of wine was passed around the table four times. The Boy asked his father the meaning of all these things, and the father repeated the story of the saving of the first-born sons of Israel in that far-off night of terror and death when they came out of Egypt. While the supper was going on, hymns were sung, and when it was ended they all chanted together:

> "*Oh, give thanks to the Lord, for He is good;*
>
> *For His loving-kindness endureth for ever.*"

So the Boy lay down under his striped woollen cloak of blue and white and drifted toward sleep, glad that he was a son of Israel, but sorry when he thought of the thousands of little lambs and the altar floor splashed with red. He wondered if some day God would not give them another way to keep that feast.

The next day of the festival was a Sabbath, on which no work could be done. But the daily sacrifice of the Temple, and all the services and songs and benedictions in its courts, continued as usual, and there was a greater crowd than ever within its walls. As the Boy went thither with his parents they came to a place where a little house was beginning to burn, set on fire by an overturned lamp. The poor people stood by, wringing their hands and watching the flames.

"Why do they not try to save their house?" cried the Boy.

The father shook his head. "They can do nothing," he answered. "They follow the teaching of the Pharisees, who say that it is unlawful to put out a fire on the Sabbath, because it is a labor."

A little later the Boy saw a cripple with a crutch, sitting in the door of a cottage, looking very sad and lonely.

"Why does he not go with the others," asked the Boy, "and hear the music at the Temple? That would make him happier. Can't he walk?"

"Yes," answered the father, "he can hop along pretty well with his crutch on other days, but not on the Sabbath, for he would have to carry his crutch, and that would be labor."

All the time he was in the Temple, watching the procession of priests and Levites and listening to the music, the Boy was thinking what the Sabbath meant, and whether it really rested people and made them happier.

The third day of the festival was the offering of the first-fruits of the new year's harvest. That was a joyous day. A sheaf of ripe barley was reaped and carried into the Temple and presented before the high altar with incense and music. The priests blessed the people, and the people shouted and sang for gladness.

The Boy's heart bounded in his breast as he joined in the song and thought of the bright summer begun, and the birds building their nests, and the flowers clothing the hills with beautiful colors, and the wide fields of golden grain waving in the wind. He was happy all day as he walked through the busy streets with his parents, buying some things that were needed for the home in Nazareth; and he was happy at night when he lay down under an olive-tree beside the tent, for the air was warm and gentle, and he fell asleep under the tree, dreaming of what he would see and do to-morrow.

III. HOW THE BOY WAS LOST

Now comes the secret of the way he was lost—a way so simple that the wonder is that no one has ever dreamed of it before.

The three important days of the Passover were ended, and the time had come when those pilgrims who wished to return to their homes might leave Jerusalem without offense, though it was more commendable to remain through the full seven days. The people from Nazareth were anxious to be gone—they had a long road to travel—their harvests were waiting. While the Boy, tired out, was sleeping under the tree, the question of going home was talked out and decided. They would break camp at sunrise, and, joining with others of their countrymen who were tented around them, they would take the road for Galilee.

But the Boy awoke earlier than any one else the next morning. Before the dawn a linnet in the tree overhead called him with twittering songs. He was rested by his long sleep. His breath came lightly. The spirit of youth was beating in his limbs, His heart was eager for adventure. He longed for the top of a high hill—for the wide, blue sky—for the world at his feet—such a sight as he had often found in his rambles among the heights near Nazareth. Why not? He would return in time for the next visit to the Temple.

Quietly he stepped among the sleeping-tents in the dark. A footpath led through the shadowy olive-grove, up the hillside, into the open. There the light was clearer, and the breeze that runs before the daybreak was dancing through the grass. The Boy turned to the left, following along one of the sheep-trails that crossed the high, sloping pastures. Then he bore to the right, breasting the long ridge, and passed the summit, running lightly to the eastward until he came to a rounded, rocky knoll. There he sat down among the little bushes to wait for sunrise.

Far beyond the wrinkled wilderness of Tekoa, and the Dead Sea, and the mountain-wall of Moab, the rim of the sky was already tinged with silvery gray. The fading of the stars travelled slowly upward, and the brightening of the rose of dawn followed it, until all the east was softly glowing and the deep blue of the central heaven was transfused with turquoise light. Dark in the gulfs and chasms of the furrowed land the night lingered. Bright along the eastern peaks and ridges the coming day, still hidden, revealed itself in a fringe of dazzling gold, like the crest of a long mounting wave. Shoots and flashes of radiance sprang upward from the glittering edge. Streamers of rose-foam and gold-spray floated in the sky. Then over the barrier of the hills the sun surged royally-crescent, half-disk, full-orb—and overlooked the world. The luminous tide flooded the gray villages of Bethany and Bethphage, and all the emerald hills around Bethlehem were bathed in light.

The Boy sat entranced, watching the miracle by which God makes His sun to shine upon the good and the evil. How strange it was that God should do that—bestow an equal light upon those who obeyed Him and those who broke His law! Yet it was splendid, it was King-like to give in that way, with both hands. No, it was Father-like—and that was what the Boy had learned from his mother—that God who made and ruled all things was his Father. It was the name she had taught him to use in his prayers. Not in the great prayers he learned from the book—the name there was Adonai, the Lord, the Almighty. But in the little prayers that he said by himself it was "my Father!" It made the Boy feel strangely happy and strong to say that. The whole world seemed to breathe and glow around him with an invisible presence. For such a Father, for the sake of His love and favor, the Boy felt he could do anything.

More than that, his mother had told him of something special that the Father had for him to do in the world. In the evenings during the journey and when they were going home together from the Temple, she had repeated to him some of the words that the angel-voices had spoken to her heart, and some of the sayings of wise men from the East who came to visit him when he was a baby. She could not understand all the mystery of it; she did not see how it was going to be brought to pass. He was a child of poverty and lowliness; not rich, nor learned, nor powerful. But with God all things were possible. The choosing and calling of the eternal Father were more than everything else. It was fixed in her heart that somehow her Boy was sent to do a great work for Israel. He was the son of God set apart to save his people and bring back the glory of Zion. He was to fulfil the promises made in olden time and bring in the wonderful reign of the Messiah in the world—perhaps as a forerunner and messenger of the great King, or perhaps himself—ah, she did not know! But she believed in her Boy with her whole soul; and she was sure that his Father would show him what to do.

These sayings, coming amid the excitements of his first journey, his visit to the Temple, his earliest sight of the splendor and confusion and misery of the great city, had sunken all the more deeply into the Boy's mind. Excitement does not blur the impressions of youth; it sharpens them, makes them more vivid. Half-covered and hardly noticed at the time, they spring up into life when the quiet hour comes.

So the Boy remembered his mother's words while he lay watching the sunrise. It would be great to make them come true. To help everybody to feel what he felt there on the hilltop—that big, free feeling of peace and confidence and not being afraid! To make those robbers in the Jordan valley see how they were breaking the rule of the world and burning out their own hearts! To cleanse the Temple from the things that filled it with confusion and pain, and drive away the brawling buyers and sellers who were spoiling his Father's great house! To go among those poor and wretched and sorrowful folks who swarmed in Jerusalem and teach them that God was their Father too, and that they must not sin and quarrel any more! To find a better way than the priests' and the Pharisees' of making people good! To do great things for Israel—like Moses, like Joshua, like David—or like Daniel, perhaps, who prayed and was not afraid of the lions—or like Elijah and Elisha, who went about speaking to the people and healing them—

The soft tread of bare feet among the bushes behind him roused the Boy. He sprang up and saw a man with a stern face and long hair and beard looking at him mysteriously. The man was dressed in white, with a leathern girdle round his waist, into which a towel was thrust. A leathern wallet hung from his neck, and he leaned upon a long staff.

"Peace be with you, Rabbi," said the Boy, reverently bowing at the stranger's feet. But the man looked at him steadily and did not speak.

The Boy was confused by the silence. The man's eyes troubled him with their secret look, but he was not afraid.

"Who are you, sir," he asked, "and what is your will with me? Perhaps you are a master of the Pharisees or a scribe? But no—there are no broad blue fringes on your garments. Are you a priest, then?"

The man shook his head, frowning. "I despise the priests," he answered, "and I abhor their bloody and unclean sacrifices. I am Enoch the Essene, a holy one, a perfect keeper of the law. I live with those who have never defiled themselves with the eating of meat, nor with marriage, nor with wine; but we have all things in common, and we are baptized in pure water every day for the purifying of our wretched bodies, and after that we eat the daily feast of love in the kingdom of the Messiah which is at hand. Thou art called into that kingdom, son; come with me, for thou art called."

The Boy listened with astonishment. Some of the things that the man said—for instance, about the sacrifices and about the nearness of the kingdom—were already in his heart. But other things puzzled and bewildered him.

"My mother says that I am called," he answered, "but it is to serve Israel and to help the people. Where do you live, sir, and what is it that you do for the people?"

"We live among the hills of that wilderness," he answered, pointing to the south, "in the oasis of Engedi. There are palm-trees and springs of water, and we keep ourselves pure, bathing before we eat and offering our food of bread and dates as a sacrifice to God. We all work together, and none of us has anything that he calls his own. We do not go up to the Temple nor enter the synagogues. We have forsaken the uncleanness of the world and all the impure ways of men. Our only care is to keep ourselves from defilement. If we touch anything that is forbidden we wash our hands and wipe them with this towel that hangs from our girdle. We alone are serving the kingdom. Come, live with us, for I think thou art chosen."

The Boy thought for a while before he answered. "Some of it is good, my master," he said, "but the rest of it is far away from my thoughts. Is there nothing for a man to do in the world but to think of himself—either in feasting and uncleanness as the heathen do, or in fasting and purifying yourself as you do? How can you serve the kingdom if you turn away from the people? They do not see you or hear you. You are separate from them—just as if you were dead without dying. You can do nothing for them. No, I do not want to come with you and live at Engedi. I think my Father will show me something better to do."

"Your Father!" said Enoch the Essene. "Who is He?"

"Surely," answered the Boy, "He is the same as yours. He that made us and made all that we see—the great world for us to live in."

"Dust," said the man, with a darker frown—"dust and ashes! It will all perish, and thou with it. Thou art not chosen—not pure!"

With that he went away down the hill; and the Boy, surprised and grieved at his rude parting, wondered a little over the meaning of his words, and then went back as quickly as he could toward the tents.

When he came to the olive-grove they were gone! The sun was already high, and his people had departed hours ago. In the hurry and bustle of breaking camp each of the parents had supposed that the Boy was with the other, or with some of the friends and neighbors, or perhaps running along the hillside above them as he used to do. So they went their way cheerfully, not knowing that they had left their son behind. This is how it came to pass that he was lost.

IV. HOW THE BOY WENT HIS WAY

When the Boy saw what had happened he was surprised and troubled, but not frightened. He did not know what to do. He might hasten after them, but he could not tell which way to go. He was not even sure that they had gone home; for they had talked of paying a visit to their relatives in the south before returning to Nazareth; and some of the remaining pilgrims to whom he turned for news of his people said that they had taken the southern road from the Mount of Olives, going toward Bethlehem.

The Boy was at a loss, but he was not disheartened, nor even cast down. He felt that somehow all would be well with him; he would be taken care of. They would come back for him in good time. Meanwhile there were kind people here who would give him food and shelter. There were boys in the other camps with whom he could play. Best of all, he could go again to the city and the Temple. He could see more of the wonderful things there, and watch the way the people lived, and find out why so many of them seemed sad or angry, and a few proud and scornful, and almost all looked unsatisfied. Perhaps he could listen to some of the famous rabbis who taught the people in the courts of the Temple and learn from them about the things which his Father had chosen him to do.

So he went down the hill and toward the Sheep Gate by which he had always gone into the city. Outside the gate a few boys about his own age, with a group of younger children, were playing games.

"Look there," they cried—"a stranger! Let us have some fun with him. Halloo, Country, where do you come from?"

"From Galilee," answered the Boy.

"Galilee is where all the fools live," cried the children. "Where is your home? What is your name?"

He told them pleasantly, but they laughed at his country way of speaking and mimicked his pronunciation.

"Yalilean! Yalilean!" they cried. "You can't task. Can you play? Come and play with us."

So they played together. First, they had a mimic wedding-procession. Then they made believe that the bridegroom was killed by a robber, and they had a mock funeral. The Boy took always the lowest part. He was the hired mourner who followed the body, wailing; he was the flute-player who made music for the wedding-guests to dance to.

So readily did he enter into the play that the children at first were pleased with him. But they were not long contented with anything. Some of them would dance no more for the wedding; others would lament no more for the funeral. Their caprices made them quarrelsome.

"Yalilean fool," they cried, "you play it all wrong. You spoil the game. We are tired of it. Can you run? Can you throw stones?"

So they ran races; and the Boy, trained among the hills, outran the others. But they said he did not keep to the course. Then they threw stones; and the Boy threw farther and straighter than any of the rest. This made them angry.

Whispering together, they suddenly hurled a shower of stones at him. One struck his shoulder, another made a long cut on his cheek. Wiping away the blood with his sleeve, he turned silently and ran to the Sheep Gate, the other boys chasing him with loud shouts.

He darted lightly through the crowd of animals and people that thronged the gateway, turning and dodging with a sure foot among them and running up the narrow street that led to the sheep-market. The cries of his pursuers grew fainter behind him. Among the stalls of the market he wound this way and that way like a hare before the hounds. At last he had left them out of sight and hearing.

Then he ceased running and wandered blindly on through the northern quarter of the city. The sloping streets were lined with bazaars and noisy workshops. The Roman soldiers from the castle were sauntering to and fro. Women in rich attire, with ear-rings and gold chains, passed by with their slaves. Open market-places were still busy, though the afternoon trade was slackening.

But the Boy was too tired and faint with hunger and heavy at heart to take an interest in these things. He turned back toward the gate, and, missing his way a little, came to a great pool of water, walled in wit, white stone, with five porticos around it. In some of these porticos there were a few people lying upon mats. But one of the porches was empty, and here the Boy sat down.

He was worn out. His cheek was bleeding again, and the drops trickled down his neck. He went down the broad steps to the pool to wash away the blood. But he could not do it very well. His head ached too much. So he crept back to the porch, unwound his little turban, curled himself in a corner on the hard stones, his head upon his arm, and fell sound asleep.

He was awakened by a voice calling him, a hand laid upon his shoulder. He looked up and saw the face of a young woman, dark-eyed, red-lipped, only a few years older than himself. She was clad in silk, with a veil of gauze over her head, gold coins in her hair, and a phial of alabaster hanging by a gold chain around her neck. A sweet perfume like the breath of roses came from it as she moved. Her voice was soft and kind.

"Poor boy," she said, "you are wounded; some one has hurt you. What are you doing here? You look like a little brother that I had long ago. Come with me. I will take care of you."

The Boy rose and tried to go with her. But he was stiff and sore; he could hardly walk; his head was swimming. The young woman beckoned to a Nubian slave who followed her. He took the Boy in his big black arms and so carried him to a pleasant house with a garden.

There were couches and cushions there, in a marble court around a fountain. There were servants who brought towels and ointments. The young woman bathed the Boy's wound and his feet. The servants came with food, and she made him eat of the best. His eyes grew bright again, and the color came into his cheeks. He talked to her of his life in Nazareth, of the adventures of his first journey, and of the way he came to be lost.

She listened to him intently, as if there were some strange charm in his simple talk. Her eyes rested upon him with pleasure. A new look swept over her face. She leaned close to him.

"Stay with me, boy," she murmured, "for I want you. Your people are gone. You shall sleep here to-night—you shall live with me and I will be good to you—I will teach you to love me."

The Boy moved back a little and looked at her with wide eyes, as if she were saying something that he could not understand.

"But you have already been good to me, sister," he answered, "and I love you already, even as your brother did. Is your husband here? Will he come soon, so that we can all say the prayer of thanks-giving together for the food?"

Her look changed again; her eyes filled with pain and sorrow; she shrank back and turned away her face.

"I have no husband," she said. "Ah, boy, innocent boy, you do not understand. I eat the bread of shame and live in the house of wickedness. I am a sinner, a sinner of the city. How could I pray?"

With that she fell a-sobbing, rocking herself to and fro, and the tears ran through her fingers like rain. The Boy looked at her, astonished and pitiful. He moved nearer to her, after a moment, and spoke softly.

"I am very sorry, sister," he said; and as he spoke he felt her tears falling on his feet. "I am more sorry than I ever was in my life. It must be dreadful to be a sinner. But sinners can pray, for God is our Father, and fathers know how to forgive. I will stay with you and teach you some of the things my mother has taught me."

She looked up and caught his hand and kissed it. She wiped away her tears, and rose, pushing back her hair.

"No, dear little master," she said, "you shall not stay in this house—not an hour. It is not fit for you. My Nubian shall lead you back to the gate, and you will return to your friends outside of the city, and you will forget one whom you comforted for a moment."

The Boy turned back as he stood in the doorway. "No," he said. "I will not forget you. I will always remember your love and kindness. Will you learn to pray, and give up being a sinner?"

"I will try," she answered; "you have made me want to try. Go in peace. God knows what will become of me."

"God knows, sister," replied the Boy gravely. "Abide in peace."

So he went out into the dusk with the Nubian and found the camp on the hillside and a shelter in one of the friendly tents, where he slept soundly and woke refreshed in the morning.

This day he would not spend in playing and wandering. He would go straight to the Temple, to find some of the learned teachers who gave instruction there, and learn from them the wisdom that he needed in order to do his work for his Father.

As he went he thought about the things that had befallen him yesterday. Why had the man dressed in white despised him? Why had the city children mocked him and chased him away with stones? Why was the strange woman who had been so kind to him afterward so unhappy and so hopeless?

There must be something in the world that he did not understand, something evil and hateful and miserable that he had never felt in himself. But he felt it in the others, and it made him so sorry, so distressed for them, that it seemed like a heavy weight, a burden on his own heart. It was like the work of those demons, of whom his mother had told him, who entered into people and lived inside of them, like worms eating away a fruit.

Only these people of whom he was thinking did not seem to have a demon that took hold of them and drove them mad and made them foam at the mouth and cut themselves with stones, like a man he once saw in Galilee. This was something larger and more mysterious-like the hot wind that sometimes blew from the south and made people gloomy and angry—like the rank weeds that grew in certain fields, and if the sheep fed there they dropped and died.

The Boy felt that he hated this unknown, wicked, unhappy thing more than anything else in the world. He would like to save people from it. He wanted to fight against it, to drive it away. It seemed as if there were a spirit in his heart saying to him, "This is what you must do, you must fight against this evil, you must drive out the darkness, you must be a light, you must save the people—this is your Father's work for you to do."

But how? He did not know. That was what he wanted to find out. And he went into the Temple hoping that the teachers there would tell him.

He found the vast Court of the Gentiles, as it had been on his first visit, swarming with people. Jews and Syrians and foreigners of many nations were streaming into it through the eight open gates, meeting and mingling and eddying round in confused currents, bargaining and haggling with the merchants and money-changers, crowding together around some group where argument had risen to a violent dispute, drifting away again in search of some new excitement.

The morning sacrifice was ended, but the sound of music floated out from the enclosed courts in front of the altar, where the more devout worshippers were gathered. The Roman soldiers of the guard paced up and down, or leaned tranquilly upon their spears, looking with indifference or amused contempt upon the turbulent scenes of the holy place where they were set to keep the peace and prevent the worshippers from attacking one another.

The Boy turned into the long, cool cloisters, their lofty marble columns and carved roofs, which ran around the inside of the walls. Here he found many groups of people, walking in the broad aisles between the pillars, or seated in the alcoves of Solomon's Porch around the teachers who were instructing them. From one to another of these open schools he wandered, listening eagerly to the different rabbis and doctors of the law.

Here one was reading from the Torah and explaining the laws about the food which a Jew must not eat, and the things which he must not do on the Sabbath. Here another was expounding the doctrine of the Pharisees about the purifying of the sacred vessels in the Temple; while another, a Sadducee, was disputing with him scornfully and claiming that the purification of the priests was the only important thing. "You would wash that which needs no washing," he cried, "the Golden Candlestick, one day in every week! Next you will want to wash the sun for fear an unclean ray of light may fall on the altar!"

Other teachers were reciting from the six books of the Talmud which the Pharisees were making to expound the law. Others repeated the histories of Israel, recounted the brave deeds of the Maccabees, or read from the prophecies of Enoch and Daniel. Others still were engaged in political debate: the Zealots talking fiercely of the misdeeds of the house of Herod and the outrages committed by the Romans; the Sadducees contemptuously mocking at the hopes of the revolutionists and showing that the dream of freedom for Judea was foolish. "Freedom," they said, "belongs to those who are well protected. We have the Temple and priesthood because Rome takes care of us." To this the Zealots answered angrily: "Yes, the priesthood belongs to you unbelieving Sadducees; that is why you are content with it. Look, now, at the place where you let Herod hang an accursed eagle of gold on the front of Jehovah's House."

So from group to group the Boy passed, listening intently, but hearing little to his purpose. All day long he listened, now to one, now to another, completely absorbed by what he heard, yet not satisfied. Late in the afternoon he came into the quietest part of Solomon's Porch, where two large companies were seated around their respective teachers, separated from each other by a distance of four or five columns.

As he stood on the edge of the first company, whose rabbi was a lean, dark-bearded, stern little man, the Boy was spoken to by a stranger at his side, who asked him what he sought in the Temple.

"Wisdom," answered the Boy. "I am looking for some one to give a light to my path."

"That is what I am seeking, too," said the stranger, smiling. "I am a Greek, and I desire wisdom. Let us see if we can get it from this teacher. Listen."

He made his way to the centre of the circle and stood before the stern little man.

"Master," said the Greek, "I am willing to become thy disciple if thou wilt teach me the whole law while I stand before thee thus—on one foot."

The rabbi looked at him angrily, and, lifting up his stick, smote him sharply across the leg. "That is the whole law for mockers," he cried. The stranger limped away amid the laughter of the crowd.

"But the little man was too angry; he did not see that I was in earnest," said he, as he came back to the Boy. "Now let us go to the next school and see if the master there is any better."

So they went to the second company, which was gathered around a very old man, with long, snowy beard and a gentle face. The stranger took his place as before, standing on one foot, and made the same request. The rabbi's eyes twinkled and his lips were smiling as he answered promptly:

"Do nothing to thy neighbor that thou wouldst not have him do to thee, this is the whole law; all the rest follows from this."

"Well," said the stranger, returning, "what think you of this teacher and his wisdom? Is it better?"

"It is far better," replied the Boy eagerly: "it is the best of all I have heard to-day. I am coming back to hear him to-morrow. Do you know his name?"

"I think it is Hillel," answered the Greek, "and he is a learned man, the master of the Sanhedrim. You will do well, young Jew, to listen to such a man. Socrates could not have answered me better. But now the sun is near setting. We must go our ways. Farewell."

In the tent of his friends the Boy found welcome and a supper, but no news of his parents. He told his experiences in the Temple, and the friends heard him, wondering at his discernment. They were in doubt whether to let him go again the next day; but he begged so earnestly, arguing that they could tell his parents where he was if they should come to the camp seeking him, that finally he won consent.

V. HOW THE BOY WAS FOUND

He was in Solomon's Porch long before the schools had begun to assemble. He paced up and down under the triple colonnade, thinking what questions he should ask the master.

The company that gathered around Hillel that day was smaller, but there were more scribes and doctors of the law among them, and they were speaking of the kingdom of the Messiah—the thing that lay nearest to the Boy's heart. He took his place in the midst of them, and they made room for him, for they liked young disciples and encouraged them to ask after knowledge.

It was the prophecy of Daniel that they were discussing, and the question was whether these things were written of the First Messiah or of the Second Messiah; for many of the doctors held that there must be two, and that the first would die in battle, but the second would put down all his enemies and rule over the world.

"Rabbi," asked the Boy, "if the first was really the Messiah, could not God raise him up again and send him back to rule?"

"You ask wisely, son," answered Hillel, "and I think the prophets tell us that we must hope for only one Messiah. This book of Daniel is full of heavenly words, but it is not counted among the prophets whose writings are gathered in the Scripture. Which of them have you read, and which do you love most, my son?"

"Isaiah," said the Boy, "because he says God will have mercy with everlasting-kindness. But I love Daniel, too, because he says they that turn many to righteousness shall shine as the stars for ever and ever. But I do not understand what he says about the times and a half-time and the days and the seasons before the coming of Messiah."

With this there rose a dispute among the doctors about the meaning of those sayings, and some explained them one way and some another, but Hillel sat silent. At last he said:

"It is better to hope and to wait patiently for Him than to reckon the day of His coming. For if the reckoning is wrong, and He does not come, then men despair, and no longer make ready for Him."

"How does a man make ready for Him, Rabbi?" asked the Boy.

"By prayer, son, and by study of the law, and by good works, and by sacrifices."

"But when He comes He will rule over the whole world, and how can all the world come to the Temple to sacrifice?"

"A way will be provided," answered the old man, "though I do not know how it will be. And there are offerings of the heart as well as of the altar. It is written, 'I will have mercy and not sacrifice.'"

"Will His kingdom be for the poor as well as for the rich, and for the ignorant as well as for the wise?"

{Illustration: From a painting by Holman Junt. The Finding of Christ in The Temple}

"Yes, it will be for the poor and for the rich alike. But it will not be for the ignorant, my son. For he who does not know the law cannot be pious."

"But, Rabbi," said the Boy eagerly, "will He not have mercy on them just because they are ignorant? Will He not pity them as a shepherd pities his sheep when they are silly and go astray?"

"He is not only a Shepherd," answered Hillel firmly, "but a great King. They must all keep the law, even as it is written and as the elders have taught it to us. There is no other way."

The Boy was silent for a time, while the others talked of the law, and of the Torah, and of the Talmud in which Hillel in those days was writing down the traditions of the elders. When there was an opportunity he spoke again.

"Rabbi, if most of the people should be both poor and ignorant when the Messiah came, so ignorant that they did not even know Him, wouldn't He save them just because they were poor?"

Hillel looked at the Boy with love, and hesitated before he answered.

At that moment a man and a woman came through the colonnade with hurried steps. The man stopped at the edge of the circle, astonished at what he saw. But the woman came into the centre and put her arm around the Boy.

"My boy," she cried, "why hast thou done this to us? See how sorrowful thou hast made me and thy father, looking everywhere for thee."

"Mother," he answered, "why did you look everywhere for me with sorrow? Did you not know that I would be in my Father's house? Must I not begin to think of the things my Father wants me to do?"

Thus the lost Boy was found again, and went home with, his parents to Nazareth. The old rabbi blessed him as he left the Temple.

But had he really been lost, or was he finding his way?

THE END

Milton Keynes UK
Ingram Content Group UK Ltd.
UKHW030741071024
449371UK00006B/653